It Happened in the Old West

Remarkable Events That Shaped History

Edited by Erin H. Turner

D0964222

TWODOT®

GUILFORD, CONNECTICUT
HELENA, MONTANA

A · TWODOT® · BOOK

An imprint of Globe Pequot
An imprint and registered trademark of Rowman & Littlefield

Distributed by NATIONAL BOOK NETWORK

Copyright © 2017 by Rowman & Littlefield
Map by Alena Pearce © Rowman & Littlefield

British Library Cataloguing in Publication Information available

Library of Congress Cataloging-in-Publication Data available

ISBN 978-1-4930-2830-6
ISBN 978-1-4930-2831-3 (e-book)

∞™ The paper used in this publication meets the minimum requirements of American National Standard for Information Sciences—Permanence of Paper for Printed Library Materials, ANSI/NISO Z39.48-1992.

Printed in the United States of America

CONTENTS

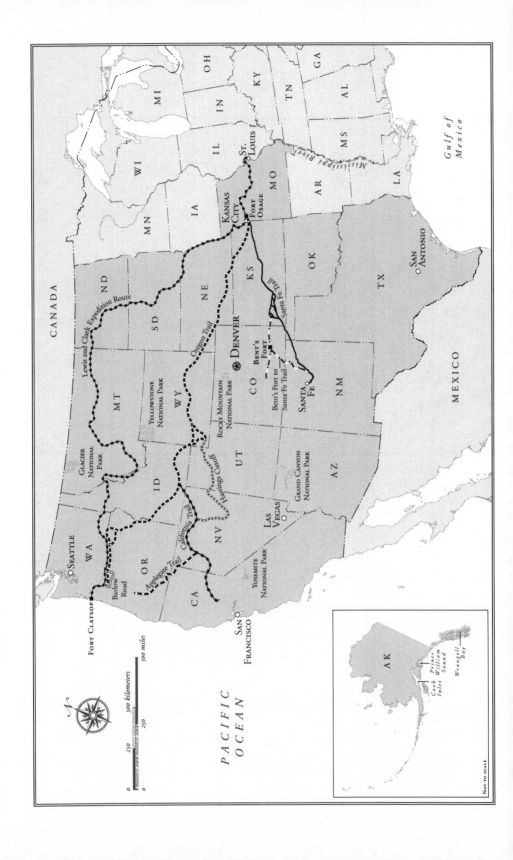

CONTENTS

CONTENTS

INTRODUCTION

These are the stories of what happened in the West as the trickle, then flood, of Easterners and immigrants first began to flow into the plains, deserts, and mountains between the Pacific Ocean and the Mississippi River and, finally, far north into the Last Frontier. While some events would have happened regardless of who was there—earthquakes, storms, droughts, and other natural disasters—it was because of this influx of humanity that those events were recorded and have become part of America's history.

The remaining balance of these events happened precisely as a result of these newcomers, and their stories go beyond the archetypal cowboy-versus-Indian battles, gold rushes, saloon shootouts, and stagecoach holdups. Many historians have noted that the communities that formed in this area during the eighteenth and nineteenth centuries often were more ethnically diverse than many large cities are today. Someone walking the streets of small towns in the Old West likely would have heard as much German, French, or Chinese spoken as English, and witnessed styles of dress ranging from chaps and cowboy boots, fancy dresses and fine suits, and buffalo robes and ornate headdresses to wooden clogs and lederhosen, silk kimonos and wide-brimmed bamboo hats, saris, and burkas.

The merging of these individuals with different religions, tongues, and economic backgrounds understandably created both tension and— for the less short-sighted—opportunities. While Native Americans often became victims of this westward expansion, others—such as newly freed slaves, immigrants, and Easterners champing at the bit for a stake to claim as their own—shaped the story and landscape of the West with their acts of courage, ingenuity, brazenness, and impudence.

Amid tales of loss and horror are accounts of survival and success. And among the countless adventurers who found the lure of wide-open spaces and untapped resources to be as strong as the Sirens' song to Odysseus, many found the determination to thrive in the West. And thrive they did—even better, for what they lacked in resources they made up in resourcefulness, becoming inventors, entrepreneurs, scientists, activists, explorers, and more. To them all we owe our gratitude for creating and recording this history as it happened in the Old West.

ALASKA

ADVENTURE ON ICE

1880

A great canoe bobbed in Wrangell Harbor, fully loaded with camping supplies. It was early August in 1880, and John Muir's eyes crackled with impatience. He was beyond ready to start his trip, but instead there he sat, waiting. Finally, Reverend Samuel Hall Young came running down the dock, with his dog behind him. After climbing into the canoe, Young called to the dog, Stickeen, and the small, black mutt leaped into the canoe and snuggled up in Young's coat.

Muir protested, saying the dog was too small to be useful and would only cause trouble, but Young refused to leave Stickeen behind. Though small, the dog was good company. The two-year-old sheltie mix had been a wedding present to Young and his wife, who were Wrangell's Presbyterian missionaries. The Wrangell natives, Stickeen Tlingits, had named the dog. Muir wanted to set off more than he wanted to argue, but he privately wondered if the dog would survive the trip.

The cedar canoe was piloted by a Wrangell guide, Lot Tyeen, who had brought with him his son-in-law, Joe, an excellent hunter and cook. Seventeen-year-old Billy, a local boy, was coming because he spoke both good English and Tlingit. Once the decision was made about bringing the dog, the five men were ready to set out.

Naturalist John Muir was not the first tourist to come to the Alaska Panhandle, but he may have been the most famous early one. His writings had appeared in American magazines, and he was known across the United States. On his first Alaskan trip the previous summer, he had met Reverend Young and they had instantly become friends. The missionary admired the naturalist's enthusiasm and stamina and asked him to stay on in Wrangell as his houseguest. Muir, in turn, talked his new friend into sharing a lengthy paddle trip that fall. The two and their guides had reached Glacier Bay before needing to return to Wrangell so Muir could make the last steamer home. Muir hadn't had nearly enough time there, and was eager to explore Glacier Bay again and take more notes. By studying Alaska's vibrant glaciers, he hoped to better understand California's small ones. This 1880 journey was a tourist trip with a serious mission.

For a map, Muir had a copy of one that had been made seventy years earlier. The coastline was drawn poorly, with few bays and glaciers marked. As they traveled, Muir corrected the lines of the map and gave names to many landmarks.

Wrangell lies halfway down the Alaska Panhandle, and Glacier Bay is more than two hundred miles to its north. The group paddled the dugout canoe north through the many islands. Muir was in a hurry to see glaciers, lots of glaciers! He pushed the men to paddle for long days. Along the way they explored narrow, glacier-carved bays called fjords. This amused the guides. Why explore a bay so icy that there was no hope of finding gold or game? Lot tied tree branches to the outer edge of his canoe to protect it from floating ice, and the men used long sticks to push away icebergs. Chunks of dense, blue ice crashed down from the steep ice walls, sending great waves across the bay. The Native Alaskan men were uncomfortable exploring so dangerously close to the ice. If they fell in, they would quickly die. Nonetheless, Muir had plotted a course and he planned to stick to it. He knew the season was short and they had to move quickly if he was going to make much progress with his map and notes.

When the party finally stopped to camp each night, Muir eagerly explored the land. Stickeen, the dog, followed him on all of his hikes. After a week, Muir admitted that he liked the dog, and the feeling was clearly mutual. Envious of their forays, Reverend Young usually stayed behind in camp since he suffered from a bad shoulder that prevented him from rock climbing.

In three weeks, the canoe reached Glacier Bay, a huge gash carved by numerous glaciers that poured down from either side. The group explored sixty miles deep into the iceberg-filled bay, stopping for a full week at grand Muir Glacier. Muir had seen and named this glacier on his 1879 trip, and it again filled him with awe.

After leaving Glacier Bay, they paddled west, coming to a smaller bay that was not on the map. The sky was thick with fog, and rain drizzled on the men, soaking them to the skin. It took all of their strength to paddle to shore through the icebergs. On the shore, they set up camp by a glacier. Muir was fascinated with this glacier: It appeared to be growing, while the others were getting smaller. Muir couldn't figure out why, and he soon declared to Young that he would spend the next day exploring the glacier, which he named Taylor Glacier.

Muir rose early and took no time for breakfast. A storm was brewing and he was in a hurry. Muir's Scottish soul loved the drama of adverse weather, and he was particularly eager to experience this glacier in a snowstorm. If the new snow fed the glacier's growth, he wanted to witness it. He dropped a biscuit in his pocket and picked up his ice ax. Stickeen insisted on joining him, though Muir told the dog to stay. Soon the two were climbing up on the ice. The sky broke for a few minutes, giving Muir a longer look at the extensive glacier, which he estimated to be eight miles wide at the water's edge. He quickly took out his notebook and drew it. The glacier was like a river of ice flowing down the mountainside, and like a flooded river, the glacier was overflowing its banks. It was uprooting trees on either side, and rocks, even great boulders, were tossed aside. It was carving the valley, just as it had carved the bay. The pressure of movement ripped the ice into great cracks called crevasses. Nature was giving him a science lesson, and Muir was a willing student.

Muir used his ax to cut steps into steep rises so that the little dog could follow him. Together, they hiked along the east bank of the glacier. This was easy enough, so he crossed the width of the glacier. The glacier center was flowing faster than the sides and was buckling into great crevasses. He figured some of these crevasses were a thousand feet deep and thirty feet across. Leaping over cracks as wide as eight feet, Muir was impressed to see the little dog follow. On the glacier's west bank, they hiked upward again. Finally, he came to an awesome lake filled with bobbing icebergs. It was beautiful, but it was getting late and time to leave.

Muir headed down, taking what he thought was the shortest route. By this time the snow was blowing harder and he wandered blindly into a maze of cracks. Muir was getting a bit nervous and wasn't entirely sure how he would get back. He had to keep his eyes trained down so he wouldn't fall into a crevasse, which concerned him since he couldn't plan a route carefully if he was always watching his feet. Nonetheless, he kept going in what he thought was the right direction, leaping over crevasses when he came to them. Stickeen leaped too. Eventually, however, the crevasses got wider, until they could not be jumped. Muir kept hoping each large crevasse would be the last. The snow was thick, night was coming, and Muir began to suspect that he would have to spend the night on the glacier.

Man and dog came to one crevasse that was much longer and wider than the others. Unable to bear the idea of trying to walk around it, Muir finally found a place where he dared to leap. Luckily, he reached the other side without sliding back into the depths. Stickeen flew across also. But the very next step posed a huge challenge. Muir was standing on an ice island. The only way off was an ice bridge that would require

Muir to climb several feet down the wall of his island, leaving him suspended in air hundreds of feet above a certain and icy death. Cutting steps with his ax, he carefully crawled down the ice bridge. As he slid along the bridge on his stomach, he flattened it with the ax. Once on the other side, Muir called for Stickeen, but the dog cried and refused to follow. Muir was amazed that the dog understood the greater danger present. After much begging from Muir, the dog stepped slowly down the ice steps to the ice bridge. Any slip would have sent him tumbling to his death. Treading slowly and whining the whole time, Stickeen finally made it to Muir. Safe! The rest of the journey down the glacier was so easy that they almost skipped with joy.

It was late when Muir and Stickeen returned to camp. They had been gone seventeen hours and were miserably cold and hungry. Muir immediately changed into dry clothes and ate a bowl of hot chowder. Once full, he told Reverend Young about their adventure and heaped praise on Stickeen.

Reverend Young had a story to tell also. The camp had had guests, a Hoonah Tlingit chief and the man's three wives. The visitors gave Young gifts of porpoise meat, salmon, clams, crabs, and strawberries. Young was amazed to see strawberries growing this far north.

Then, the visitor asked a favor. Could Reverend Young pray to his god to stop the glacier from advancing? It was blocking off a valuable salmon stream, and in a few years it would totally cover the stream. Hoping to please the glacier spirit, the chief had already killed two of his slaves. The missionary saw this story as proof that these people needed Christianity. Muir saw it as proof that the glacier was growing. Further studies would confirm to Muir that he was correct in theorizing that snow accumulation fed the glaciers and that increased precipitation would push a glacier downhill. Later scientists would establish that a steep rock bed under the glacier hastened its movement.

From Taylor Bay the group quickly paddled south. Muir was in a hurry to catch the southbound September mail ship. His canoe trip had lasted about six weeks, and he needed to return home to California.

Muir shared his map with the US government since it was much better than any other chart available at the time. Using his notes from the summer's trip, he also wrote magazine articles and books. The story of Stickeen, Alaska's brave ice-climbing dog, touched America and became the subject of his best-loved book. Glacier Bay National Park includes the glacier of Stickeen's adventure, now known as Brady Glacier.

DEATH ON THE GLACIER

1897

In the summer of 1897, George Hall came to Alaska on a mission. He was looking for his friend, Charles Blackstone. Hall had made a promise to Blackstone's wife to find his friend, dead or alive.

Charles Blackstone had come down with "gold fever" the year before, and eventually his dreams of striking it rich in Alaska were too much to resist. Leaving his wife and children at home in Seattle, Blackstone headed north, fully expecting to return home a rich man. He asked his friend Hall to watch after his family if he failed to return in the fall.

In late April 1896, Blackstone, along with 250 other men, climbed aboard a steamship bound for Alaska. He quickly befriended two other passengers, Charles Botcher and J. W. Malinque, who, like many on board, had never mined before. In place of experience, they each had camping supplies, shovels, picks, gold pans, and dreams.

They talked about gold—dust, flakes, and nuggets. The summer before, pounds of it had been found in a creek that fed Cook Inlet's Turnagain Arm. Everyone on the ship was sure that he would soon be rich too.

The ship arrived in Cook Inlet in early May, when the area was still in the grip of winter. The inlet was thick with chunks of ice, and the captain refused to travel up to Turnagain Arm. Instead, he anchored near the mouth of the inlet, some two hundred miles from the gold streams. His crew would row the passengers ashore in longboats, but this was the end of the line for the ship. On the beach, there was still thick snow, but even so there was already one mining party camping there. These miners told the newcomers how hard it could be to travel in this wild country and warned them that although the melting snow was a hassle, it wouldn't get much easier after the snow was gone. The Kenai Peninsula was a rain forest, and it was crisscrossed with streams, swamps, glaciers, and mountains. Walking through this maze was difficult at best. Boating up the inlet was not much easier. Some days the water shot through Turnagain Arm like a thirty-foot wave; the miners weren't kidding when they called this tide the "cannonball," as it shot back any boat that tried to muscle past it.

While on Turnagain Arm, the men explored the main mining camps, optimistically called Hope City and Sunrise City. A trading post was being set up in each new location, giving the camps a stamp of respectability. The men were somewhat puzzled that there were large Native Alaskan villages elsewhere on Cook Inlet, but not on Turnagain Arm. It would be some time before they figured out that the Athabaskans knew Turnagain Arm had the worst boating on the inlet.

Mulling over all this information, the newcomers weighed their options. They had to decide quickly what they were going to do, since the captain was readying the ship to return to Seattle for another load of miners. Did anyone want to leave Alaska yet? Blackstone, Botcher, and Malinque, along with the majority of the other men, said no. Although things looked rough, they were not quitting. The second question was easier to answer: Did anyone want to send a letter back to Seattle? There might not be another chance to send a letter home, so many of the men quickly jotted down their news and well wishes to their loved ones.

Other ships arrived in Cook Inlet and the tent camp at the inlet's mouth kept growing. Men were restless to get to the Turnagain Arm gold. Some cut down trees, sawed boards, and built crude boats and hand-carved oars. Hundreds hoped to row the two hundred or so miles around the inlet.

One day, Botcher and a few others crept away from the camp and into the woods. They followed a river deep into the center of the Kenai Peninsula. There, they dipped their gold pans into creeks and swirled them until only the heaviest sand and a few gold flakes lay in the bottom. Flakes! One could not get rich working for a few flakes! Botcher had counted on gold nuggets and was sorely disappointed. The summer was passing fast and things did not look promising.

Rumors were flying up and down Cook Inlet. There were stories of fifty-dollar gold pans. There was also news of empty rowboats and bodies washed ashore. One unhappy miner wrote this little poem on a scrap of paper:

> *In God we trusted, In Alaska we busted, Let her rattle:*
> *Will try it again in old Seattle.*

Blackstone, Botcher, and Malinque gave up on Cook Inlet. In late summer, they left to look for gold up on the Yukon River. News of the Circle goldfield was enticing, but they had missed the last Yukon River steamship of the season, and the thousand-mile hike proved too much for the three. Discouraged, they were back on Turnagain Arm in March, poorer than they had been when they left.

Of the 3,000 gold miners on Turnagain Arm over the summer, there were only 300 left, including the 150 men wintering at Sunrise City. A year earlier, the camp had not even been a trading post, but in 1897 the boomtown had several stores, a brewery, two saloons, and two restaurants. Despite the comforts, the three men did not want to stay. Their funds were greatly depleted, their spirits were low, and they were tired of Alaska. Blackstone knew that his family would be worried about him.

Getting back to Seattle would not be easy, since no ships came to Sunrise City in the winter. Turnagain Arm was a ship captain's nightmare in winter: It was shallow, which meant that it froze, broke up, and froze again with each tide. On the other hand, deep Prince William Sound flowed all winter. To obtain winter passage on a ship, one had to hike to the sound.

The men of Sunrise City provided instructions on how to hike to Prince William Sound, as many of them had made the trip themselves. They also warned Botcher and his friends to watch out for fog and blizzards—both were common and could be deadly. They would also have to watch for great cracks in the ice, large enough to swallow a man forever. When they reached Portage Glacier, they were to follow the trail marked with stakes and ropes. If the men stayed on the marked trail, they should make it safely to the trading post at Portage Bay, where they could wait for the next ship south.

In Sunrise City, the Blackstone party packed with care. Their dog, Spot, was tied to a sled, which was piled high with food and blankets and covered with a moose hide. Ladders were lashed to the side and would serve as bridges if they needed to cross a wide crack in the ice. The men offered to carry letters to Seattle. A few letters, hoarded for months, were added to the load. On the morning of March 25, the three men left Sunrise City. Spot pulled the sled, while one man pulled its gee pole and another pushed from behind. Two days later, two men traveling to Sunrise saw the Blackstone party on Portage Glacier. Soon after this, however, a blizzard rose up, and Blackstone's group never reached the Portage Bay trading post.

Back in Seattle, Blackstone's wife feared the worst. George Hall took it upon himself to travel to Cook Inlet to find out what had happened. People in Sunrise City told him they remembered his friend, and directed Hall to follow the trail to Portage Glacier. He spent a fair amount of time on the glacier, searching for clues, footprints, and lost gear. Most of the footprints followed the rope trail, but not all. A few went off to the right, and Hall followed these. They went on and on, eventually wandering off of Portage Glacier. Not sure where to search next, he followed a mountain ridge for a long time, and then dropped down on a new glacier. Under a ledge of ice, he found the body of his friend Charles Blackstone. Poor Charles's face and hands were black with frostbite. Pinned to his chest was this handwritten note:

> *Saturday, April 4th, 1897—This is to certify that Botcher froze to death on Tuesday night. J. W. Malinque died on Wednesday forenoon, being frozen so badly. C. A. Blackstone had his ears, nose, and four fingers on his right hand and two on his left hand frozen an inch back. The storm drove us on before it. It overtook us within an hour of the summit and drove us before it. It drove everything we had over the cliff except blankets and moose hide, which we all crawled under. Supposed to have been forty degrees below zero.*
>
> *On Friday I started for Salt Water. I don't know how I got there. Have enough grub for ten days, providing bad weather does not set in. Spot was blown over the cliff. I think I can hear him howl once in a while.*

While unimaginable luck had brought Hall to Blackstone's body, he was not able to find the bodies of Botcher and Malinque, nor did anyone else report finding them. Hall sent a letter to Mrs. Blackstone reporting on his sorry discovery, and the story appeared in the Seattle newspaper that summer. Ironically, Hall had been bitten by gold fever and decided to stay on in Cook Inlet. That fall, he staked his own Turnagain Arm gold claim. Unfortunately, his creek was not very productive.

The Prince William Sound glacier where George Hall found his friend's body was named Blackstone Glacier. It feeds Blackstone Bay, where the shore is usually wrapped in fog or blowing snow. The wind still howls like a forsaken dog.

ARIZONA

THE ORDEAL OF
THE OATMAN GIRLS

1851

Royce Oatman must have been a bit uneasy on this March day in 1851. After all, he, his wife Mary Ann, and their seven children had left their farm in northern Illinois far behind them. After months of torturous travel, they had reached the hostile Indian territory of the Southwest, spurred on by the dream of building a utopian community on the banks of the Colorado River.

The Oatmans had left Independence, Missouri, in the summer of 1850, as part of a train of twenty wagons, fifty people, and a herd of cattle. At the direction of the Mormon leader James Brewster, the party planned to establish a "New Zion" near what is now the border between California and Arizona.

The Oatmans eventually left the wagon train along with two other families, the Wilders and the Kellys. For almost a month, they all lingered at a friendly Pima Indian village on the Gila River, northwest of Tucson. Now, Oatman was anxious to move on—so anxious that he chose to begin the last leg of this difficult journey without the Wilders and the Kellys. He was apprehensive about this decision to go it alone.

On March 19, as the Oatman wagons creaked along the Gila River about eighty miles east of its confluence with the Colorado, they met a small party of Yavapai Indians who asked for tobacco and bread. Although the Oatmans had little to spare, Royce complied. But the Indians demanded even more food. Afraid he would not be able to feed his family, Oatman refused.

Instantly, the Yavapai attacked the wagon train and killed everyone except fifteen-year-old Lorenzo, who was left for dead; his fourteen-year-old sister Olive; and a younger sister, Mary Ann. The two terrified girls were taken captive.

At the Yavapai village, the girls were treated roughly by the Indian women and put to work as slaves. Lorenzo was rescued by passing emigrants and taken to Fort Yuma, California, where he recovered from his wounds. Eventually, he gravitated to San Francisco. He worked ceaselessly to free his sisters from the Indians.

Sometime in early 1852, the Yavapai sold Olive and Mary Ann to a party of Mojave Indians, who lived about 150 miles up the Colorado River from Fort Yuma. The Mojaves treated the frightened girls with more kindness than the Yavapai. Olive later recalled:

> *We were conducted immediately to the home of the chief,*
> *and welcomed with the staring eyes of collecting groups*
> *and an occasional smile from the members of the chief's*
> *family, who gave the warmest expressions of joy. . . . The*
> *chief's house was a beautiful but small elevation crowning*
> *the river bank, from which the eye could sweep a large*
> *section of the valley and survey the entire village, a portion*
> *of which lined each bank of the stream.*

Even though life was easier with the Mojaves, Olive and Mary Ann still dreamed of being free again. After months of captivity, Mary Ann died of malnutrition. Olive was fully adopted into the tribe, even having her face tattooed in the traditional manner of Mojave women.

In 1855, Henry Grinnell, a civilian employee at Fort Yuma, learned that the Mojaves had a white woman living in their village. He approached Lieutenant Colonel Martin Burke, the commandant of the fort, with a plan to rescue Olive. Grinnell suggested that a Yuma Indian named Francisco, who was friendly with the Mojaves, should go to their village and attempt to ransom the girl. On January 27, 1856, Burke wrote the following letter, which Francisco carried on his mission:

> *"Francisco, Yuma Indian, bearer of this, goes to the
> Mohave Nation to obtain a white woman there, named
> Olivia [sic]. It is desirable that she should come to this
> post, or send her reasons why she does not wish to come."*

Francisco succeeded in bringing Olive to Fort Yuma. After five years among the Indians, the young woman had almost forgotten English, but in time she recovered both mentally and physically from her ordeal. Lorenzo, now living in Los Angeles, immediately headed for Fort Yuma and a long-awaited reunion with his sister.

Olive became an overnight celebrity. With Lorenzo, she toured California and met Royal B. Stratton, a minister who volunteered to act as her publicist. In 1857, Stratton published a book, *Life among the Indians: Being an Interesting Narrative of the Captivity of the Oatman Girls.* The book became an instant best seller and was reissued several times over the next few years under the title *Captivity of the Oatman Girls.*

Stratton's book is part of a distinct genre of American historical literature called "Indian Captivities." There are hundreds of such narratives depicting the plights of unfortunate whites taken prisoner by various Indian tribes, from the earliest settlement of America to the late nineteenth century. James Levernier and Hennig Cohen, two modern compilers, in their book *The Indians and Their Captives*, make the following interesting point:

> *After the Revolutionary War, when Indians became the main obstacle to frontier expansion, the captivity narratives became almost exclusively a device for anti-Indian propaganda. A few narratives presented a sympathetic picture of Indian life, but most were shaped by publishers exploiting a mass market that thrived on sensationalism, in a natural alliance with land speculators who wanted to implement a policy of Indian extermination in the interest of real estate development. Accounts like . . . R. B. Stratton's Captivity of the Oatman Girls . . . among dozens of others, were designed to horrify audiences into hating what the novelist Hugh Henry Brackenridge . . . an editor of captive narratives, referred to as "the animals, vulgarly called Indians. . . ." In them, the Indian is painted so irredeemably brutish that he deserves to be deprived of his lands.*

Olive eventually married John B. Fairchild in New York, lived in Michigan for a few years, and finally moved with her husband and children to Sherman, Texas. She died in 1903. Lorenzo died in Nebraska in 1901.

THE BRIEF SUCCESS OF
THE OVERLAND MAIL

1858

John Butterfield was a man of vision. From humble beginnings as a New York stagecoach driver, he had built a successful mail service in that state, increasing his fortune along the way. He was also prominent in real estate and banking circles, and at one time he served as mayor of Utica, New York.

But it is not for his success as a New York politician and businessman that Butterfield is remembered today. Rather, his fame stems from his organization and leadership of the Overland Mail Company.

In the late 1850s, California was still a remote outpost of the United States. Although the region's population had grown significantly since statehood in 1850, an enormous distance separated it from the East. There were only three ways to cross that distance: First, there was the long, difficult overland journey, which could take weeks or even months. Second, there was the sea journey from an eastern port to Central America, then overland across Panama or Nicaragua, and then by sea again up the coast to California. And finally, there was the sea journey around the tip of South America. Obviously, none of the routes provided a timely way of transporting the US mail.

In March 1857, Congress passed legislation authorizing the creation of an overland mail service. Bids were let to various entrepreneurs, and in September the contract was awarded to the Overland Mail Company, an establishment formed by John Butterfield and several associates. For six hundred thousand dollars a year, the firm agreed to provide mail service twice a week from Memphis and St. Louis to San Francisco and Los Angeles. The contract required that each delivery be completed in less than twenty-five days.

For the next year, the Overland Mail Company spent more than a million dollars exploring a route, building way stations, buying coaches and equipment, and hiring drivers and other employees. Finally, on September 14, 1853, the first mail run started cross-country from San Francisco. It arrived in St. Louis twenty-four days, eighteen hours, and twenty-six minutes later. In the meantime, the westbound run had left St. Louis on September 16. It arrived in San Francisco in twenty-three days, twenty-three hours, and thirty minutes.

In Arizona, the Overland Mail Company route followed much of the earlier wagon road blazed by Colonel Philip St. George Cooke. The primary difference was that the mail route entered Arizona from New Mexico several miles farther north, to take advantage of Apache Pass. The trail passed through Tucson and then turned north, generally following the Gila River to its confluence with the Colorado at Yuma.

Way stations along the route were about twenty miles apart. Those in Arizona were built of stone or adobe. Each station was manned by about six to eight employees whose duties were to care for the horses and mules and to be sure a fresh team was ready for the stage when it arrived. For the comfort of any passengers who might be aboard, a fresh coach was provided every three hundred miles.

Butterfield's motto was, "Remember, boys, nothing on God's earth must stop the United States mail." To live up to his maxim, he hired only the best men for the job and bought only the best livestock available. According to Waterman L. Ormsby, a correspondent at the time for the New York *Herald*, Butterfield's employees were without exception "courteous, civil, and attentive." Most of them were from the East, he noted, and many were from New York. "I found the drivers on the whole, fine and with few exceptions experienced men," he said. "All the superintendents are experienced men."

Of the horses that pulled the heavy coaches, Ormsby wrote, "[They] are of the most powerful description to be found, and when once thoroughly trained to the service perform the laborious run with apparent pleasure and delight." In Arizona, mules were usually substituted for the horses because they were better suited to the terrain.

The Overland Mail Company employed close to two thousand men and operated about two hundred way stations along its 2,800-mile route between the Mississippi River and the Pacific Ocean. With the onset of the Civil War, the company closed its southern road and shifted most of its activity farther north.

The Overland Mail Company was one of the most massive undertakings of its time. However, despite strong financial backing, brilliant leadership, and excellent planning, it was doomed to fail. It was simply too big and too expensive. By the time Butterfield was replaced as company chairman in 1860, the rival Pony Express had made its debut. Telegraph lines and railroad tracks would soon span the continent. The Overland Mail Company was a victim of progress.

GRAND CANYON

THE CRUEL COLORADO

1889

Today few end up dead or severely injured when running the Colorado River through the Grand Canyon. Sure, going down the Colorado is not as safe as, say, reading a book—paper cuts and strained vision notwithstanding. But thousands of people run the Colorado every year nowadays, and the vast majority come bobbing along a week or two later, leaving the canyon with exhilarating memories and a kinship to groovers but few lasting negative effects.

Robert Brewster Stanton and his crew suffered mightily in their first and second attempts at running the Colorado to the river's mouth at the Gulf of California in 1889–1890. An engineer by training, Stanton sought to survey the river to determine if a railroad could be built through the canyon. Although Stanton survived the two attempts and later wrote of the multiple disasters they faced in a matter-of-fact, unemotional style, his crew and his benefactor did not leave the canyon unscathed. Three did not leave the canyon at all.

In March 1889 Frank M. Brown, a wealthy Denver-based entrepreneur, formed the Denver, Colorado Canyon and Pacific Railroad.

He had no train engines, no tracks, no coal cars—but he had a vision. Coal drove the steam engines that drove the economy of Brown's day, and the western slope of the Rocky Mountains in Colorado had lots and lots of coal. Mountains and canyons stood between those productive coal mines and the infant but growing cities of Los Angeles and San Francisco, making the construction of a railroad line through the canyon country to California highly problematic. But when consulting a map of the region, one route stood out: the Colorado River through the Grand Canyon. With a relatively tame gradient (compared to going over mountains and in and out of canyons) and a direct route (as perceived while standing back a few feet from the map), the river canyon was the "perfect" solution to his can't-get-the-lucrative-coal-to-the-people-who-will-pay-big-money-for-it problem. Engineers had built railroads through very difficult terrain, and the time-honored solution to impassable mountains was to have the tracks follow river canyons. To Brown, a railroad through the Grand Canyon was a no-brainer. But first, the route needed to be surveyed.

Brown hired Stanton as the official surveyor of the river party, and to help attract investors, Brown decided to lead the exploration team himself to show how easy it was to go down the Colorado. Brown personally planned the trip, ordering five lightweight, narrow, short, cedar boats (the intention being to avoid the ponderous portages Powell had faced with the weighty craft he employed). He did not order any life preservers for himself, Stanton, or the other fourteen members of his crew.

When the crew loaded their boats at Green River, Utah Territory (farther down the Green and wholly separate from Green River, Wyoming, where the Powell expedition began), it quickly became apparent that the boats were not big enough to carry all of the supplies. Thinking quickly, the team built a raft out of driftwood and loaded the remaining supplies onboard, to be towed behind the boat of George Gibson and Henry Richards, Stanton's servants. Seemed like a good idea at the time. They left Green River on May 25, 1889.

In Cataract Canyon in south-central Utah Territory, some eighty miles downriver from their starting point, the first rapid destroyed the raft and two of the crew's five boats. Supplies, cedar planks, and men spun and roller-coastered through the rapid; although all survived, the loss of the boats and most of their supplies crippled the expedition. And they hadn't even reached the Grand Canyon.

Stanton, four men, one boat, and some meager supplies (a few chunks of bread, coffee containing largely river water, some sugar, and a little condensed milk) stayed behind. They would work their way down the rapid, while Brown and the rest of the crew shot ahead to get supplies at Hite, or "Dandy Crossing," one of the mining camps in Glen Canyon. Drinking a lot of water to feel full, Stanton's men took six days to get through the forty-one river miles of Cataract Canyon. As they emerged, weak and disgruntled, the crew met three men hauling supplies upriver for them. Temporarily rejuvenated, they pushed on to Dandy Crossing to meet Brown and his men.

Not surprisingly, three crew members quit the expedition at the mining camp, but Brown hired a mountain man, Harry McDonald, to shore up his disintegrating crew. Skilled at carpentry, the newest crewmember quickly got the party's remaining boats "river-worthy," and the crew pushed on to Lees Ferry in Arizona Territory. Thankfully, 150 miles of relatively tame water in Glen Canyon coddled the expedition, and they arrived at Lees Ferry on July 2, content and unscathed.

Brown rented a horse and rode ninety miles to Kanab, Utah Territory, to get supplies. He returned seven days later, and the expedition decided to push on with three overloaded boats and eight men (including Brown, Stanton, and the photographer Franklin A. Nims), the goal being to get quickly through Grand Canyon but not to survey the route: Nims's images would serve Brown's purposes of attracting investors.

The night of July 9, the expedition camped at Soap Creek Rapid, in Marble Canyon (today part of Grand Canyon National Park), ten miles below Lees Ferry. The next morning, Brown confided in Stanton that he had dreamed about rapids for the first time since the trip began. This was probably of passing interest to Stanton at the time, but, within minutes of launching the boats, reality and Brown's inner dream world merged.

Brown's leading boat plunged into the tempest of Soap Creek Rapid. Stanton followed, but almost immediately hit big water, only to see Brown's boatmate, Harry McDonald, waving frantically from shore. After running the rapid and pulling into an eddy, Stanton could hear McDonald, who shouted, "Brown is in there!" By "there" McDonald meant a whirlpool in the rapid. Looking back, Stanton saw nothing, except for Brown's notebook, floating in his direction. They scooped it out of the water, but Brown himself was never seen again.

The crew spent the day searching for Brown to no avail, and then set up camp for the night. Sad but not overly sentimental, the engineer Stanton wrote, "In this world we are left but little time to mourn." He and the remaining members of his team pushed off the next morning.

Over the next five days, they ran or portaged around twenty-four rapids. The twenty-fifth (ironically known today as 25-Mile Rapid) killed two more men, Peter Hansbrough and Henry Richards. Their boat became pinned under a low, overhanging ledge and overturned; both men drowned.

This was too much. As Stanton wrote, "Astonished and crushed by their loss, our force too small to portage our boats, and our boats entirely unfit for such work, I decided to abandon the trip." They camped one more night and cached supplies in a cave (today known as Stantons Cave) above the waterline, seeking shelter themselves as a storm rocked the canyon. It was not a pleasant night's sleep. "I have seen the lightning play," Stanton wrote, "and heard the thunder roll among the summit peaks of the Rocky Mountains, as I have stood on some rocky point far above the clouds, but nowhere has the awful grandeur equaled that night in the lonesome depths of what was to us death's cañon."

The next day they hiked out to the North Rim via South Canyon and eventually reached a Mormon cattle ranch. The settlers gave the beat-up explorers a wagon ride into Kanab, and Stanton was back in Denver in a few days' time. Immediately, he began planning a return trip.

On November 25, 1889, Stanton and his crew of eleven men (four returning from the previous year's disaster) pushed off from the mouth of Crescent Creek just above Dandy Crossing in Glen Canyon. Stanton had learned much from the year before, and he outfitted the expedition with longer, wider, deeper oak boats with sealed compartments to keep the boats afloat if they should capsize, cork life preservers for the crew, and watertight rubber bags for supplies.

When they reached Soap Creek Rapid where Brown had drowned, they were surprised to see how tame the river seemed, although they knew the river was nine feet lower than it had been during their last attempt. However, as Stanton would soon find out, big water wasn't the only danger on the Colorado.

On January 1, 1890, the photographer, Franklin Nims, fell from a cliff, plummeting twenty-two feet to the rocks below. He was alive, but quite beat up, including a broken leg just above the ankle. They spent the night nearby and pushed off the next morning, with Nims on a stretcher made of canvas drawn out between oars, to search for a way out of Marble Canyon and get the photographer some medical attention.

They found a route at Rider Canyon. Stanton and two men climbed out, and Stanton hiked thirty-five miles back to Lees Ferry to get help. The other men returned to the river to help bring Nims out. The next day the men began the ascent with Nims on the stretcher. At times, they hauled the photographer over scree slopes at an angle of forty-five degrees and up huge boulders blocking the route. They made it to the rim, but had not planned on spending the night, so they had brought few supplies. Soon it began to snow. They built a fire and fed their remaining provisions—a few pieces of chocolate dissolved in hot water—to Nims.

Stanton returned with a wagon the next morning, and Nims was taken back to Lees Ferry. Sixteen days later he reached Winslow, Arizona Territory, with a group of Mormons headed that way. A doctor there treated not only his broken leg, but several more broken or dislocated bones and a fracture at the base of his skull. Nims survived.

The eleven remaining men returned to the river and resumed the expedition. On January 17 they found the body of Peter Hansbrough, one of the crew members who had drowned on the previous expedition. They buried his remains the next morning. "The burial service was brief and simple," Stanton wrote. "We stood around the grave while one short prayer was offered, and we left him with a shaft of pure marble for his headstone, seven hundred feet high, with his name cut upon the base; and in honor of his memory we named a magnificent point opposite," today's Point Hansbrough.

Finally, mercifully, the tragedies came to an end. The rest of the trip was still rough but not deadly, although one crewmember, Harry McDonald, left the expedition and hiked out to the North Rim when he had had enough. Stanton and the remaining nine pushed on, eventually reaching Diamond Creek, where they could hike out and get provisions at Peach Springs, Arizona Territory. They took a break there and didn't launch again until late February. They reached the Sea of Cortez on April 26, 1890.

Ironically, although Stanton left the Colorado River with a firm conviction that a railroad could be built through the Grand Canyon, oil had since been discovered in California, and his backers refused to fund a railroad with the principal purpose of hauling coal.

NORTHERN CALIFORNIA

GOLD FROM THE AMERICAN RIVER!

1848

On the morning of January 24, 1848, James Marshall quietly reported to work at the site of the new sawmill that had been built in the site he had chosen on the South Fork of the American River. A new arrival to California, Marshall, who was a sober man from New Jersey, had been assigned to choose the site of the mill and supervise its building by John Sutter, a German who had come to what was then Mexican California by way of Switzerland. Having gone bankrupt in his adopted country, Sutter determined that California was the Promised Land and he headed there intending to start a utopian empire for himself called Nueva Helvetia or New Helvetia.

On his way to California, Sutter had stopped for a time in Hawaii, and it was rumored that he brought several Hawaiian women with him to his new home as concubines. It was certainly not a rumor that he had many Indians working for him at his new location and that they were kept in a state of semi-slavery.

Luckily for Sutter, when he arrived in California in 1839, a colony of Russians at Fort Ross near Bodega Bay had just been given orders from the czar that they were to sell off their holdings and abandon their colony. They offered their goods to Sutter for thirty thousand dollars, and he accepted the offer, on the condition that he could pay it off over a long period. When the deal was struck, he built Sutter's Fort at the confluence of the American and Sacramento Rivers, to be the center of his empire.

Sutter had become quite successful with his method of empire building, and especially with his trading post at a site forty-five miles from the sawmill, which traded with the many emigrants who were coming to California from the United States. Encouraged by the influx of settlers from the United States and seeing economic opportunity at every turn, Sutter decided to enter the lumber business and he hired Marshall to help him do it. Variously described as brooding and eccentric, Marshall actually enjoyed his work very much and was delighted with the progress that had been made on the sawmill by his crew of Native Americans, Mormon veterans of the recent war between the United States and Mexico, and a family of settlers named Wimmer.

Marshall was not one to share his excitement, but he might have conveyed his disappointment in early January 1848, when the machinery was about to be installed in the mill and they discovered that the lower end of the tailrace that turned the main water wheel was not deep enough. Marshall ordered the men to blast out the section of river, making a deeper channel for the water to travel through.

When he arrived at the site on the morning of January 24, Marshall was again pleased with the progress that had been made. He stepped down the bank to look at the deeper tailrace made by the blast and admired the work that had been done. Then he spotted a few shiny particles—of what, he wasn't sure—in the water.

The men were curious about the particles, but not too impressed. Marshall was cautious about making too much of the find before he knew for sure what it was. He gathered the pieces and set off for Sutter's Fort and the trading post to discuss the matter with his employer.

Once back at Sutter's Fort, Sutter and Marshall devised every test they could think of to determine if the samples were actually what Marshall suspected they were—gold. Eventually, they concluded that while the pieces seemed to be genuine, the find at Coloma was probably not a large one. Even so, they agreed, it would be best to officially obtain title to the land where the gold had been found, and they dispatched an employee to procure the necessary paperwork from the military governor at Monterey.

Marshall returned to the mill with his news, but the men seemingly remained unimpressed; only a few spent their spare time panning in the water, hoping for another find. When the work on the mill was complete, however, most of the workers remained in the area to be joined by friends with whom they had shared the news of the gold discovery. A few more samples were found, but the men remained calm, quiet, and satisfied to keep the news to themselves. One of the most important events in California's history had just happened in the water at their feet, but it would take some time for the world to find out about it.

The employee who had been sent to obtain the land grant at Monterey was sworn to secrecy about the find, but when he reached the village of Benecia, where the population was excited about the discovery of coal at Mount Diablo, he felt he had to share his even more exciting news. At San Francisco, the employee even showed his sample to an experienced gold miner, but still everyone he met remained relatively unimpressed.

In March, two San Francisco newspapers ran stories about the gold discovery, and Sutter himself was interviewed—but he continued to play down the importance of the discovery. In the meantime, just a few hundred prospectors had come into the area, and Sutter was making a fairly good living trading with them. He had no real need to hope for an expansion of the find, but he also dabbled in the mining business, employing Native Americans to do the digging for him. Life at Sutter's Fort and in California remained relatively unchanged.

Then, almost in an instant, it would never be the same again. A man named Sam Brannan, a prominent merchant in Sutter's New Helvetia colony who was interested in increasing his own business, ran frantically through the streets of San Francisco with a bottle full of gold dust on about May 12, yelling "Gold! Gold! Gold from the American River!" Apparently the fervent cry of the man and his rapid pace finally excited the town's interest. By June 1, three-fourths of the population of San Francisco had left for Sutter's Fort. San Jose was practically deserted, and towns up and down the coast, as far south as Santa Barbara and Los Angeles, emptied as well.

But the biggest rush was yet to come. In his State of the Union address in December 1848, President James K. Polk announced the discovery, and the news of the strike was officially out. Soon the news had spread around the globe, and in 1849 the rush for gold in California was officially on!

James Marshall never made much money from the gold he discovered in the American River—he sold his interest in the mill for two thousand dollars, and then boasted that he knew of even richer deposits elsewhere. The miners who heard this announcement at the mill threatened to hang him unless he shared the location of the other cache. He managed to escape, but the mob tore the mill to bits.

Marshall's employer, John Sutter, was given credit for the discovery by the government and even received a pension because of it. Sutter's dreams of a utopian New Helvetia and massive wealth were ended by the Gold Rush, however. His fields were overrun by the mobs of miners who came to the area, ending his plans for an agricultural empire, and he was unable to find any workers to run the businesses at the fort. Everyone, it seemed, had gold fever—and neither Sutter, ever the opportunist, and Marshall, the discoverer, was able to profit from it. Even Sutter's scheme to use Native American miners and keep the lion's share of the profits for himself eventually failed. It was ironic that this man who had so encouraged and hoped for emigration had been ruined by it. His legacy lives on in California, however; the little fort he started did grow into a fine city, and it is now the capital of California, Sacramento.

THE HEAD OF JOAQUIN MURIETA

1852

A large crowd gathered outside the sheriff's office that hot, dusty afternoon in the small town of Stockton, California. The office had just received word from the state legislature that a reward was being offered for the capture of the notorious outlaw Joaquin Murieta. The sign a deputy was now hanging on a tree bearing the words DEAD OR ALIVE offered a reward in the amount of five thousand dollars for the capture of the outlaw.

Suddenly, the crowd parted and a rough-looking stranger with a prominent pistol at his side elbowed his way through. He brazenly strode up to the tree, took a pencil from his pocket, and carefully lettered, "I will pay $1,000 myself. J. Murieta." No one in the shocked crowd stopped the outlaw, who simply mounted his waiting horse and rode out of town again.

In the lawless early days of California, Joaquin Murieta was an outlaw legend. Many considered him a modern-day Robin Hood, who shared his takings with fellow Latin Americans who were persecuted in California in the years following the Mexican-American War. In the war, the United States had acquired the land that became the State of

California from Mexico, and many emigrants who had come to the new state from the eastern United States were in favor of denying the rights of citizenship to Latin American residents, even if they had been there first. As a result, many Latin Americans were forced off of their land by the whites.

Joaquin Murieta had a mighty rage against the gringos, or white Americans, who were taking over northern California. He was not completely unjustified in his anger, nor was he alone in his feelings.

Murieta had been born in Sonora, Mexico, and had drifted north to California with a circus as a young man with his wife Rosita. A brother of Murieta's joined them later, and the two of them staked a rich claim in Stanislaus County during the Gold Rush. Successful and happy in their new life in California, the brothers became the unwitting targets of less-successful American miners who were jealous of their success. A group of Americans beat Joaquin Murieta nearly to death, raped Rosita, and murdered his brother. Later, accused of stealing his own horse in his attempt to get away, Murieta was flogged until he collapsed in agony.

In the years after the attack against his family, Murieta became an outlaw who traveled and marauded with his wife Rosita, who wore her hair cut short and was more than handy with a pistol. They had a sidekick, Three Finger Jack, who was also known as Manuel García. The three were among the first true stagecoach robbers in the West, and they never hesitated to murder innocent travelers or to raid settlements and camps if they thought money was to be had.

Murieta and his family were not the only Mexicans to receive ill treatment at the hands of the gringos. Because of this, during their three-year career, the Murieta gang could gather up to eighty men—all of whom had been outraged, robbed, and beaten by the gringos—to fight the whites at any given time.

It was said that Joaquin Murieta was taking revenge on all of the men who had harmed his family. It was also said that when he did capture one of the men who had been involved, he frequently tied the man by a rope to his saddle horn and dragged him behind his horse to his death. But Murieta's fury knew no bounds; it extended even to the innocent Chinese miners in the area, whom he would capture, tie together in groups of a half-dozen or more, and slit their throats. Murieta had become a cold-blooded killer. Clearly, he had to be stopped.

Though he escaped the law many times, even on that bold day in Stockton, Murieta was eventually betrayed by a friend named William Burns, who led a posse of twenty-five men on a raid to the outlaws' camp at Tulare Lake. Three Finger Jack and Joaquin Murieta were both killed when they were awakened from a sound sleep next to a campfire by the gunshots of their attackers. The posse received the reward money, by now up to six thousand dollars.

Joaquin Murieta's head and Three Finger Jack's hand were removed by an opportunistic member of the posse, who proudly displayed them in San Francisco preserved in a jar of whiskey. He shared his treasure with the curious in San Francisco for the admission price of one dollar. The head was regarded almost as a religious icon by some superstitious Mexican supporters of Murieta's crusade. Some of the more superstitious among them claimed that it even continued to grow hair.

Many people, including Rosita, Murieta's long-suffering wife and partner, declared that the head was not his at all. She claimed that Murieta had escaped to Mexico with a herd of horses and fifty thousand dollars, and other friends of his in northern California would testify to seeing him alive years after his supposed capture and death.

His head, whether real or a hoax, wasn't the only thing that remained of Murieta in California. He was the stuff of legend, and the stories of his deeds still abound today. In fact, almost all of the stories about Joaquin Murieta are just that, legend, including the story of his bold strides into Stockton. There were a number of outlaws in California at the time he was supposed to have been terrorizing settlers and stagecoach drivers who also took credit for Murieta's deeds, and no one really knows who was responsible for all of them.

SAN FRANCISCO

HALLIDIE'S HILL CLIMBER

1873

San Francisco's typical summer fog hovered low in the streets just as it was getting light. On this day, August 2, 1873, inventor and industrial designer Andrew S. Hallidie was ready to test out his latest and most risky invention. A few people were about in the drizzle, curious to see if Hallidie's horseless carriages that he called cable cars could defy gravity on a hill.

Hallidie had hired a gripman to operate the contraption on its inaugural ride along the 307-foot-long, 20 percent grade of Clay Street between Jones and Kearny Streets. The gripman was to grab and pull a long, upright handle in the middle of the car, called the grip, that connected to a continuously moving cable beneath the street. Hallidie said the action would move the car forward. To stop, Hallidie instructed the gripman to release the grip.

What the gripman, trained as a locomotive engineer, hadn't counted on was that Hallidie intended to face the car apparatus *down* the hill. The pull of gravity would add to the gripman's challenges. Another challenge was the two-part cable car. The sixteen-passenger traction car with the grip was called a "dummy," while a fourteen-passenger car connected to it was the "trailer."

Hallidie was under pressure. San Francisco supervisors had granted him a permit to try out his "Wire Rope Street Railway," as he called it, by August 1. It was now August 2, and having missed the legal deadline, Hallidie was desperate to succeed. Later, Hallidie would claim that the feat was accomplished on August 1.

Scotsman Andrew Smith Hallidie had arrived in San Francisco in 1852, twenty-one years earlier. The Gold Rush was in high gear and Hallidie used metal wire rope technology that his father had already patented in Scotland to make wire rope for suspension bridges and for Northern California mining operations. As he traveled, surveyed, and built bridges, Hallidie discovered a need for a continually moving pulley. He fine-tuned a metal cable ropeway to haul equipment in California's mines. Hallidie was granted a patent for an "endless cable ropeway" in 1867.

Two years later, Hallidie was standing at the corner of Kearny and Jackson Streets. The city was noisy with passenger carriages, trams clattering over cobblestones, and whinnying horses pulling wagons with heavy loads of supplies to stores and businesses.

As he watched the bustle of traffic, Hallidie heard something and glanced west up the Jackson Street Hill. Sounds of clattering and crashing wood mixed with the terrified neighs of horses falling backward. The wagon, pulled by a five-horse team, was too heavy to make it up the slope. The horses lost their balance and became trapped in the rigging.

The horrifying event that Hallidie witnessed was not uncommon on San Francisco's hills. Supplies were damaged or destroyed, and in the worst-case scenarios, horses and people were injured or killed. Tram horses were lucky to survive four years. A shocked but observant Hallidie believed he could come up with a solution.

San Francisco attorney Benjamin H. Brooks was already working on a cable railway to solve the hill transport problem. Along with some partners and an engineer, he obtained a cable line franchise in 1870 that would allow a line to extend west several miles from downtown San Francisco. The partners were unable to secure financing, so Brooks, barely able to spare time from a successful law practice, and his team eventually sold the franchise rights to Hallidie.

Hallidie spent the next years and more than sixty thousand dollars constructing what local papers called "Hallidie's Folly." He chose the steep, six-block-long Clay Street Hill for his testing ground. Two 150-horsepower steam engines fueled by coal in a nearby powerhouse would move the eleven thousand feet of underground wire cable along the Clay Street Hill.

Hallidie waited for the gripman to mount the dummy car. But the gripman was staring down narrow, forty-nine-foot-wide Clay Street to Portsmouth Square, six steep blocks below. The crowd knew something was wrong. The cable car should be on its way by now if it was going to move at all. This test would prove whether Hallidie had built a runaway mechanical hazard, or, if he was as good a designer as he claimed, a cable car that might make life easier and safer. If he didn't act soon, the day's regular traffic would start making its way up the hill.

Hallidie leaped to the grip as the gripman turned his back and left the scene. If the cable car had been a horse, Hallidie would have seized the reins, since it could be considered equivalent to a mechanical horse. The cable car was under control! Hallidie gripped and released as he inched the double-car conveyance forward, down to the first intersection at Mason Street. The cable car leveled out, as it would do at every street crossing to come.

Hallidie had proven the cable car's worth. Immediately the Clay Street Hill Railroad began carrying passengers, including the mayor, up and down the hill. The Clay Street line would be extended west to Van Ness Avenue in 1877. Hallidie became wealthy from the five-cent fares.

More cable railway lines would be constructed, including one up the California Street Hill by the rich residents of Nob Hill. In 1882 all cable cars added bells to warn pedestrians and horses. Turntables were installed for the major lines to turn cars around 180 degrees so that a car need only go in one direction. By 1900, cable cars were operating in twenty-eight American cities.

But the cable cars' San Francisco heyday, with nine companies operating six hundred cars over twenty-two lines, lasted barely three decades. Cheaper electric streetcars with overhead wires were introduced in 1892 and became the city's choice for rebuilding transportation systems after the 1906 Earthquake and Fire. Most cable-car lines, including Hallidie's, were abandoned.

In 1947, Mayor Roger Lapham told San Francisco supervisors, "The city should get rid of its cable cars as soon as possible." Friedel Klussmann, known as the Cable Car Lady, rallied women's and civic groups to save the quaint cable cars as a tourist draw, and voters agreed. In 1964, San Francisco's Cable Cars became a moving National Historic Landmark.

YOSEMITE NATIONAL PARK

WATERFALL ON FIRE

1874

One night during the spring of 1874, Yosemite visitors were treated to an extraordinary spectacle—a waterfall seemingly caught on fire! James McCauley, owner of the new Mountain House Hotel atop Glacier Point, had made a habit of building a large campfire each evening for his summertime guests. They would sit around the fire, laugh, sing, tell stories, and warm their hands and toes until almost bedtime. One night after everyone had gone back inside the hotel to escape the gathering mountain chill, McCauley decided to clean up the hotel grounds by kicking the remains of the campfire over the cliff. Apparently, many of the coals were still live since they flared up as they fell more than half a mile down to the bare rocks at the base of the cliff.

The long, bright streaks of flame caught the eyes of many campers and nighttime strollers down in the valley. Everyone who saw it was delighted by the spectacle. To many it seemed as if the whole side of the cliff was lit up in a spray of flame. Some said it looked as if one of Yosemite's waterfalls had caught on fire.

When McCauley heard of this unexpected response, he decided to intentionally re-create what Yosemite visitors started to call the "Firefall" each and every night. He saw this as a way of attracting attention to his hotel and as a means of earning a little extra money. Each day McCauley's twin sons, John and Fred, were sent into the valley to solicit donations from park visitors, who gladly gave small sums to keep the spectacle alive. McCauley reciprocated by putting on the very best show he could manage.

Since, in those days, there was no set time for the event, McCauley would wave a flaming torch back and forth as a signal to spectators that the Firefall was about to begin. McCauley continued this tradition for more than fifteen years, but it was interrupted in 1897 when the innkeeper lost control of his hotel to a competing hotel owner from Wawona. For several years after that, Yosemite visitors who had seen it in the past were disappointed when they looked up toward Glacier Point in the evening and saw no campfire, no torch, and no Firefall.

In 1899 David Curry established a large public camping facility near the foot of the 3,200-foot Glacier Point cliffs. Curry heard glowing descriptions of McCauley's Firefalls from campground guests, and eventually he decided to stage the event himself. On holidays and other special occasions, he sent campground employees to the top of the cliffs to gather dry sticks, twigs, bark, and other kindling. At nightfall these combustibles were set on fire, allowed to burn down to glowing embers, and then dumped over the edge.

On those nights when a Firefall was scheduled, campground guests and other spectators waited with growing anticipation while the fire was built atop the cliffs. In this case the only signal that the Firefall was about to begin was David Curry's booming voice—so strong that it could be heard from the cliffs half a mile overhead—giving the command to let the show begin. The playful Curry readily admitted that he had a loud voice, so loud in fact, that he sometimes referred to himself as Captain Stentor, after the famous Greek herald whose commands, it is said, could be heard by an entire army. After warming up the crowd with a few well-chosen jokes and a story or two, Curry, in his guise as Captain Stentor, would look upward toward the cliff tops and shout, "Let'er go!"

The effect of Curry's Firefalls proved even more spectacular than those that McCauley had created during the 1880s and 1890s. The bright red and yellow streaks of flame often reached from the top of Glacier Point all the way down to the rocks at the base of the cliffs. Many attempted to take photographs of the Firefall, and images of it can be found in more than a few century-old vacation scrapbooks.

However, while campground guests and other park visitors took great delight in the Firefall and in Curry's antics, the United States Park Service was not amused. In 1913 park officials ordered Curry to stop putting on his Firefall show. Curry complied under protest and thereafter described Camp Curry as the place "where the Stentor calls and the fire used to fall."

By this time the Yosemite Firefalls had become world-famous, and visitors arriving at the park invariably asked about it. Rangers grew tired of disappointing them, and in a few years the Park Service reversed its no-Firefall policy. The shows were reintroduced during the 1917 summer season just as the US troops began heading off to join their World War I allies in Europe, where they would see fireworks of a distinctly different sort.

Thereafter, the Firefall became an established Yosemite summertime tradition, and the show began each evening at 9:00 sharp. In Camp Curry, as the embers began to tumble down the face of the Glacier Point cliff, campers would sing the "Indian Love Call." At other campgrounds around the valley, they would usually sing "America the Beautiful."

The Firefall and many other traditional Yosemite Valley activities were discontinued during World War II. Some park service officials felt the Firefall was an inappropriate distraction in a natural area such as Yosemite and argued that the nightly performances should not be resumed after the war. However, they were overruled, largely because visitors wanted to see the show.

Postwar prosperity made it possible for more and more young families to own automobiles and take long vacations. Many picked popular national parks such as Yellowstone and Yosemite as destinations. Since the Firefall was especially exciting and attractive to children, it contributed to the family entertainment aspect of the park's offerings. However, more than a few visitors came to Yosemite Valley specifically to see the Firefall, and this added to the rapidly increasing problem of overcrowding. By the mid-1960s Yosemite rangers and park officials had had enough. In 1968 National Park Service Director George Herzog ordered the Firefalls stopped, and they have not been seen since.

SOUTHERN CALIFORNIA

AN ATMOSPHERE OF SUSPICION

1871

Kuang Kao and Heng Huo wanted to get married. The young lovers had come to America from China. They owed the cost of their passage to separate *tongs*, organizations that had brought them across the Pacific Ocean. The problem was that the two young Chinese owed loyalty to rival tongs, each of which guarded its turf ferociously. Though the pair swore they were in love, their sponsoring groups would hear of no such union.

The two immigrants had begun their romance on the crowded streets of Chinatown in Los Angeles, where posters lettered in inky characters proclaimed goods for sale. Chinatown extended along both sides of Alameda Street and housed more people per square foot than any other part of the city. The English- and Spanish-speaking citizens of Los Angeles had little to do with the Chinese quarter, visiting it only if they wanted exotic goods: green tea, embroidered shawls and handkerchiefs, candied ginger, even opium. Left mostly to themselves, the Chinese lived by the rules of the two tongs that governed the area.

Kuang Kao and her new lover had tried to escape from those who claimed to own them by running away to Santa Barbara. But the leaders of Chinatown would not be denied. They determined to bring the pair back, and to use the American legal system to do it. The bosses told the police that Kuang Kao was a notorious criminal. They were on hand to mock her when she stepped from the train at San Pedro in custody. Eventually, the charges against Kuang Kao were dropped.

Then Heng Huo planned an even better ruse. Why not get married the American way, enlisting the double forces of law and church on their side? In a small chapel, Kuang Kao became Heng Huo's wife and a member of his clan. That night, Chinatown exploded. Shots burst from open windows, fireworks exploded at all hours, and angry voices argued in the alleys. The Chinese tongs fussed and boiled. No one was injured, but the air throbbed with noise of ire and celebration.

Just outside the Chinese section, the residents of greater Los Angeles fidgeted. Something was going on in Chinatown; signs of vice were more pronounced than usual. The police, already tired of the section's intrigues, chafed at the sounds of pistol fire. Even if they had known the lovers' story, the Angelenos would not have been inclined toward sympathy. Most thought all Chinese were immoral and not entitled to the protection of the law.

The codes of the Chinese tongs were indecipherable to mainstream Los Angeles, and its residents did not want to understand them. The language barrier made it hard for the small number of Chinese workers to blend into the larger population. Most non-Asian people thought that the Chinese made few efforts to become culturally American. The courts wouldn't have allowed them full legal rights anyway. In the "Yellow Peril" legislation of the time, Chinese were excluded from US citizenship.

In this atmosphere of suspicion, something unexpected happened. On the night of October 24, 1871, police entered the Chinese quarter to break up an argument between members of the tongs. By whim or by accident, someone in the Chinese section killed a white policeman. Shots were fired, and one hit officer Robert Thompson. Fellow officers carried him to a nearby drugstore, where he died. The policemen responded to the murder of one of their own with something worse than murder: organized vigilante action. Mobs of non-Asian men grabbed guns and ropes and descended on the now quiet Chinese streets. In the next five grisly hours, they killed as many Chinese men as they could catch, dragging some down the street by their braided hair or with a noose. A Chinese doctor was killed for the money in his pockets and the diamond ring on his finger. In all, the mob stole forty thousand dollars from Chinatown homes and businesses. The next morning, nineteen bodies lay in a row near the jail. At most, only one of the dead men could have been accused of any wrongdoing.

Some said the war in Chinatown was started by love, but others knew it for what it was: a battle over race and money.

Despite that violent night, the Chinese continued to prosper. Even in the 1870s, when the California Gold Rush era was fizzling out to nothing, the Chinese made strides toward wealth. They fished for abalone and sold the meat to China as a delicacy; within a few years this became a million-dollar industry. The immigrants also raised vegetables, ran laundries, and worked many jobs, some in Angeleno households as domestic servants. Their merchant class grew, and their trade networks spread. Today, Chinese and other Asian immigrants and their descendants make up one of the fastest-growing sectors of California's population.

A DAY OF REST

1873

The hired cook broke the seal on the oven door and lifted an aromatic stew from the still-hot coals. As she set the steaming dish before him, Joseph Newmark thought how each Saturday the warm midday meal seemed like a minor miracle: it had simmered in the cast-iron stove for nearly twenty-four hours, untouched by flame or human hands. Newmark enforced Jewish Sabbath law in his household, and said no one could perform work from Friday night until Saturday at sunset. "This will be the best *chamim* yet," Newmark pronounced from his seat at the head of the table. "Already I can taste the garlic and sweet California onions."

With a prayer of thanks, Newmark broke one of two loaves of sweet white challah bread for his guests at this most important Sabbath luncheon. The twelve friends and family members ate the spicy stew of chickpeas and beef, sopping up the best juices with the bread, in recognition of the importance of ritual. Here in the far West, they were keeping the same traditions that their forefathers had kept for thousands of years. As God himself had commanded Moses, they were reserving the seventh day of the week for rest and celebration.

For Jewish people throughout the world, every Saturday was a holy day. But this week in Los Angeles, the Sabbath luncheon was even more important: Congregation B'nai B'rith was celebrating a sign of permanence. After twenty years of growth, the small Jewish community had built its first tall, stately synagogue. Those who feasted at Newmark's table had just come from the new temple on Fort Street.

Lifting glasses of brandy, the men toasted progress made manifest in the new solid brick building. It signified stability, with leaded glass windows and heavy wooden doors. Within the new building, they and their families had assembled, men on the main floor and women in the balcony, to give thanks. They had come together this day like ingredients for the Sabbath stew, with an equally happy result.

Over his dinner, Newmark remembered less cohesive times. Like other restless young men, he had come west in 1854, intending to raise his fortune by selling supplies to miners in the Gold Rush. Selling goods came naturally to many of the young Jewish pioneers, since their ancestors had also worked in the "backpack business," trading whatever goods they could carry. Spices, furs, fabrics, precious stones—these things became their treasure when persecution in Europe drove them from place to place.

But the American frontier was not organized around the young men's religion. For instance, because kosher butchers were rare, they had to learn to prepare their own food according to dietary law. They worked Saturdays, in spite of their faith, since the adobe shops of Los Angeles stayed open. They met for worship when their work allowed, in private homes or rented spaces. Even when they could not obey all the laws of their religion, Newmark and his peers had kept the Sabbath by gathering on Friday nights to light candles and bless their shared wine.

Just this year, the Jewish men had helped found the new Chamber of Commerce, and had been called the city's "best citizens" in the local newspaper. Together with their wives and children, they formed a Hebrew Benevolent Society and purchased lots for a Jewish cemetery. As

Newmark himself was proud of noting, they shared a sense of upward mobility and a willingness to adapt.

The Jewish men and women of the City of Angels shared something else: a particularly American brand of freedom. In frontier Los Angeles, Jewish people were allowed to thrive as they seldom had in eastern or European cities. The "Israelites," as non-Jews called them, found a remarkable atmosphere of tolerance in Southern California. Unlike the Chinese, who looked so obviously different, they were not persecuted as they had been in so many places, for so many centuries. Living side by side with Catholics and Methodists, they entered the worlds of business and government. Their names could be found on the pages of the local Blue Book—a guide to the booming town—and on the membership rosters of local societies.

Now, with the completion of the Fort Street synagogue, they had made their mark on the land, too. The building was a solid and beautiful symbol of their hopes for the future. Newmark and the men at his table spoke of the temple's beauty as they basked in this day of rest. It had taken them twenty years of enterprise and hard work to build a place where they could worship. Like God, who rested on the seventh day, they felt the satisfaction of having been present at the creation.

Just after sunset at the Havdalah ceremony that ended the Sabbath day, Joseph Newmark started his new week. It was a gentle August evening. In an atmosphere rich with wine, spices, and the yellow, flickering light from a candle, the patriarch of the Los Angeles Jewish community may have imagined that California would grow once trains reached it from the East. He may have pictured the arrival of more German and, later, Russian Jews to swell his congregation's ranks. In the room's darkest shadows he may have foreseen the horrible world wars that would bring even more of his people west. But in his best dreams he could not have imagined what would one day come to pass: that Los Angeles would hold more than 150 Jewish congregations, and that by the mid-twentieth century it would be home to more Jews than anywhere in the world outside Israel and New York City.

COLORADO

THE BLAZING OF THE
GOODNIGHT-LOVING TRAIL

1866

In 1869 Charles Goodnight made an important decision. A Texas rancher and trail-driver, he was already widely known among cattlemen as the partner of Oliver Loving, one of the first men to bring Texas longhorns into Colorado Territory. But Loving had died the previous year, and now Goodnight decided to leave Texas and try his hand at organizing a ranch in southern Colorado.

As he stood on the banks of the Arkansas River, west of Pueblo, he was amazed at the absolute beauty of the spot. Here, among canyons lined with cottonwoods and box elders, he would build a herd the likes of which Colorado had never seen before. The range, watered by the melted snows of the nearby Rocky Mountains, was lush, and Goodnight's business sense told him that the thousands of cattle he would raise here would yield rich rewards when the railroad got as far as Denver.

Goodnight was just the man to build such a ranch. He had been born the day before the Alamo fell in March 1836, in far-off Illinois. He moved to Texas with his family as a lad and helped out on the poor farm that his stepfather had left Illinois to obtain. Upon reaching adulthood Goodnight became a scout and independent ranger, but at the same time, he continued learning about the vast herds of Texas longhorn cattle that seemed to be everywhere.

During the Civil War, Goodnight served the Confederacy in Texas as a ranger keeping peace with the Comanches along the frontier. When the war was over, hundreds of Texas farmers and ranchers put down their weapons and returned home to find their spreads ruined by neglect. And they found that the longhorns, in the absence of care, had multiplied many fold and were overgrazing much of the sparse range. Clearly someone needed to devise a way to market the cattle.

Even before a man named Joseph McCoy dreamed of driving Texas cattle northeastward to the newly founded railhead town of Abilene, Kansas, Goodnight and Loving were playing with the idea of driving a herd westward into New Mexico, then northward to Denver, Colorado Territory. In 1866 the two men got a sizable herd together and started west toward the Pecos River. They crossed the stream and proceeded to Fort Sumner, New Mexico Territory. After selling some of the cattle there, Goodnight returned to Texas to round up a new herd, while Loving continued on to Denver. There he sold the rest of the herd to John W. Iliff. The trail the two partners had carved from Fort Belknap, Texas, to Denver became known as the Goodnight-Loving Trail.

The following year Loving was severely wounded by Comanche Indians as the partners moved another herd along their trail. He died at Fort Sumner, but Goodnight went on and delivered the cattle to their buyers. On his way back through Fort Sumner, he had his partner's body exhumed and laid in a crudely made metal coffin. Goodnight placed the coffin in a wagon and drove it back to Texas for a proper burial, which is what his friend wished for on his deathbed.

After Goodnight returned to Colorado in 1869 to establish his ranch along the Arkansas River, he was met with rapid success. He now felt secure enough to take a wife, and the following year he went back East to marry his Tennessee-born sweetheart, Mary Ann Dyer. He brought his new bride back to Colorado, where he expected they would spend the rest of their lives together.

Goodnight became active in the community of Pueblo. He was an organizer of the town's first bank, the Stock Growers Bank of Pueblo. The future seemed bright for Goodnight and his fellow ranchers in southern Colorado, but in reality the nation was on the brink of one of the worst depressions ever to hit North America—the Panic of 1873. Goodnight and his neighbors hit rock bottom, and Goodnight later lamented that "the panic wiped me off the face of the earth."

By 1876 Goodnight's good life in Colorado was over. He took his wife and what few cattle he still owned and went back to Texas. There, in the Palo Duro Canyon, Goodnight established a new ranch. Over the next few years he was instrumental in developing and breeding new strains of domestic cattle. With an Irish immigrant named John Adair, he helped amass almost one million acres, which supported nearly one hundred thousand cattle. Their JA Ranch rapidly became one of the largest and most famous spreads in all of North America.

After Adair died, Goodnight decided to slow down and divided the JA with Mrs. Adair. "I am heartily sick of men and ranches," he wrote her. But he still maintained more than a hundred thousand acres upon which he raised cattle and some buffalo. In 1898 Goodnight and his wife founded Goodnight College. They also organized two churches in West Texas. Mary Ann Goodnight died in 1926, and Charles followed in 1929.

Texas lays claim to Charles Goodnight, and with his fame as part owner of the magnificent JA Ranch, maybe rightly so. But before he was a rancher in Texas, he was a Coloradan, and he and his spread near Pueblo were known far and wide. As his noted biographer, J. Evetts Haley, once put it, Goodnight's "force, his fearlessness, his plains-craft, and his mental vigor . . . will be remembered throughout the West as long as the story of cattle and horses intrigues the fancy of men."

THE GREAT DIAMOND HOAX

1872

Heads turned and tongues wagged as the two disheveled prospectors made their way down Powell Street in San Francisco that summer day in 1872. After all, the city was well on its way to becoming the metropolis of the Pacific Coast. One would have thought all that nasty prospecting for gold and groveling around in the dirt for silver were over. California was civilized, and the days of the Gold Rush were long gone.

But unbeknownst to the pedestrians along Powell Street, these dirty, ill-clad men were neither gold nor silver prospectors. They had something in their sack that had never before been found in North America. And when the news of what they had brought with them from Colorado spread throughout the financial district of San Francisco, a near-riot broke out.

It may have shocked the erudite San Franciscans, but it probably would have come as no surprise to the mountaineers of Colorado that diamonds, yes diamonds, had recently been discovered in their own backyard. After all, had not their territory yielded some of the most fantastic gold finds of the century, starting with the Pike's Peak gold rush that attracted more than fifty thousand prospectors by 1859? And was not silver, gold's sister metal, being extracted right this instant from the Rocky Mountains in unprecedented amounts?

The Colorado diamond craze all started that day in 1872, when the two men, Philip Arnold and John Slack, both originally from Kentucky, arrived in San Francisco and made their way to the bank at the far end of Powell Street. The two had never seen such a fancy bank before, and they spent a few moments looking about the place, while equally curious stares were directed at them.

The men finally walked up to a vacant window and pushed a heavy, dirty sack toward the wide-eyed teller. They told the man they wanted to leave the sack for safekeeping while they had a look around town. The teller called his manager, who explained that he needed to see the contents of the sack before he could take responsibility for it.

One of the old prospectors untied the leather strings that held the mouth of the sack closed. Carefully picking up the bag by the bottom, he poured its contents onto the counter. Out rolled hundreds of uncut diamonds, ranging in size from no bigger than a match head to the size of a twenty-dollar gold piece!

After a few minutes of conversation, the prospectors raked the diamonds back into the sack and again pushed the bag toward the teller, who this time cheerfully issued a claim ticket. All eyes were upon the men as they casually left the building and walked down Powell Street to see the sights of San Francisco.

It did not take long for news of the diamonds to spread like wildfire throughout the bank. Within days, everyone in San Francisco's financial community had heard the story of the two grizzled old men who had mysteriously appeared in the Bank of California with a large portion of diamonds.

Curiosity fired by greed immediately developed among the bank's officers over the origin of what appeared to be very fine diamonds. Thinking the prospectors naive and simplistic, the bankers decided they would attempt to learn the location of the diamond fields.

They approached the two prospectors, and after much talk and pleading, they "persuaded" the pair to reveal the location of their diamond mine on the premise that the bankers were interested in investing in the venture. A representative of the bank was immediately dispatched to Colorado to conduct a firsthand inspection of the diamond fields. The prospectors blindfolded him when they drew near the site, which turned out to be four days from Black Buttes, Wyoming, on a mesa in northwestern Colorado. Permitted to hunt to his heart's content, the representative was quick to find much more evidence, including rubies, that pointed to the great value of the diamond fields.

Meanwhile, back in California, after hearing the glowing report of their field representative, the bankers decided to ask Tiffany's of New York to verify the quality of the stones. The esteemed jewelry firm reported that if the diamonds were available in quantity, they would be worth a "rajah's ransom."

Within a short time of receiving all this good news, a syndicate of Californians promptly invested ten million dollars and organized the San Francisco and New York Mining and Commercial Company. The two prospectors "grudgingly" allowed themselves to be bought out for six hundred thousand dollars. After Henry Janin, a well-known mining engineer, personally inspected the diamond site and testified to its authenticity, the syndicate was barraged with requests from others trying to get in on the action. Before the mad rush was over, more than twenty-five companies had been organized, offering more than $200 million worth of stock. All had charters to exploit the diamond fields of Colorado.

Sometime later, Clarence King, who later became the first director of the US Geological Survey and who only recently had mapped the region where the diamonds were supposedly found, reported that the site had been "salted." No diamonds naturally existed there. Furthermore, a detailed investigation of the two prospectors' diamonds showed they had cutters' marks on them. Finally, a report from London revealed that the Kentucky men had purchased a quantity of inferior stones there the previous year.

Arnold and Slack had completely duped the California financiers! Millions of dollars were lost, and not one diamond was ever found! Lawsuits were filed, but what could be done? The investors had taken part in the endeavor only after they had investigated it and thought it to be perfectly legitimate.

Nobody was left smiling after the hoax was exposed except Arnold and Slack. Arnold did find it in his heart to settle partially with the hoodwinked investors out of his proceeds from the scam. But he still had enough money left to live comfortably in Kentucky until his death in 1878. The other con man retired to New Mexico, where he became a coffin-maker.

DENVER

THE GREAT FLOOD

1864

William Byers walked toward the edge of Denver City, wandering down street after street as he tried to figure out where to build the headquarters for his newspaper. When he reached Cherry Creek, a small stream with sandy beds lined by chokecherry bushes, he suddenly knew exactly where he should build: right in the middle of the creek. He would place his *Rocky Mountain News* office diplomatically between two rival towns—Denver City on one side of the creek, Auraria on the other. Sales of his newspaper wouldn't be limited in either place. Pleased by his brainstorm, Byers hurried through town, looking for someone who could sink piles into the bed of the creek and begin constructing his headquarters.

Indians and mountain men had warned gold seekers in Denver that the trickling waters of Cherry Creek could quickly turn into a raging torrent during times of heavy rain, but the settlers thought the mountain men were crazy, and they had no interest in the knowledge Native Americans had gleaned from living close to the land. Denver's citizens paid the waters of Cherry Creek little attention other than to use them as a source for panning gold. They put ramshackle buildings on the banks of Cherry Creek, and even built some structures on stilts in its bed.

The Arapaho and mountain men who saw people building in the middle of the stream scolded them, but the stubborn pioneers continued to build. Soon Cherry Creek was crammed with shacks and shanties and rickety buildings tottering on wooden stilts. Stores and offices straddled the creek. A Methodist church and a jail were constructed in the streambed. Even City Hall, in an effort to appear impartial between the feuding towns of Auraria and Denver City, followed the example of William Byers and built midstream on neutral ground. The dribbling creek alarmed none of the newcomers to the area. They noted that even in spring, when the mountain snowpack melted and rainstorms pummeled the plains, Cherry Creek rarely held more than a thin trickle of water. But this soon changed.

After Denver City and Auraria merged to become Denver, the *Rocky Mountain News* published the following when floodwaters rose along the Palmer Divide, a ridge jutting out from the Rocky Mountains southwest of Denver: "Cherry Creek appears to present a rather serious problem, for we have had a demonstration of what may be expected from a heavy rainfall on the Divide, though we are not yet inclined to believe the Indian claims that the whole settlement is subject to flood."

The debate over whether the flood danger was real or not was settled on the night of May 19, 1864. For an entire week leading up to that evening a heavy dumping of hail and rain had poured down on the mountains west of Denver. When the storm finally stopped on May 19, some citizens noticed that Cherry Creek was running higher than usual, but no one expressed concern. Other than the slowly rising waters, the coming flood gave little warning.

A few minutes before midnight, while some Denverites were in bed and others were in gambling halls, saloons, and brothels, a flash flood descended on the city. One man reported that he "heard a strange sound in the south like the noise of wind, which increased to a mighty roar as a great wall of water, bearing on its crest trees and other drift, rushed toward the settlement." The flood, which began in the upper end of the Cherry Creek watershed and in the Plum Creek drainage, reached its maximum height—some eyewitnesses said the crests of waves rose twenty feet or more—in Denver at about 2:00 a.m. on Friday, May 20. By 7:00 a.m. the waters had begun to lower. One frightened citizen of Denver described the flood this way: "It was the water engine of death dragging its destroying train of maddened waves, that defied the eye to number them, which was rushing down upon us." As the flood swept through town, moonlight and the bonfires of curious onlookers lit the destruction. Chaos ensued. "Alarm flew around, and all alike were ignorant of what to think, or say, or do, much less of knowing where to go with safety, or to save others."

Union soldiers from nearby Camp Weld built makeshift boats and navigated the rising waters, saving desperate citizens from drowning. Other concerned Denverites warned people away from the swelling stream as buildings in the bed of Cherry Creek and along its banks were smashed and swept away. The *Rocky Mountain News* headquarters was ruined; its printing press was destroyed. Printers who had worked late that night were sleeping in the building when the flood hit. They escaped by grabbing a rope thrown from shore. City Hall was devastated; its safe, containing town records and land ownership documents, was lost. The jail collapsed. One prisoner who had been freed by the flood only to find his life threatened by the rising tide grabbed hold of a passing cottonwood tree. He floated for miles downstream and was finally fished out of the swirling water. Records regarding the fate of prisoners set loose by the flood don't exist, but without a city hall to sentence them, or a jail to hold them, the liberated criminals likely went free.

Scores of businesses, churches, bridges, warehouses, stables, and outbuildings were borne away on the floodwaters. Ranches along the South Platte River were ruined. Both halves of Denver—the former Denver City on one side of Cherry Creek, Auraria on the other side—were joined in mutual destruction as several feet of water spread for miles in all directions, wiping out much of the fledgling frontier settlement. Between eight and nineteen people were reported killed by the flood, and estimates of the damage it caused, in 1864 dollars, range between $250,000 and $1,000,000. Countless citizens of Denver were left homeless and were forced to take temporary shelter in tents and wagons until new homes could be raised.

When the flood receded, it left in its wake a horrible stench from dead livestock, pools of contaminated water, acres of thick mud, and snarls and snags of debris. Fortunately, no major disease epidemics broke out. Unfortunately, however, food prices skyrocketed due to all the crops that had been destroyed and the livestock that had been killed on nearby farms and ranches.

Newspaperman William Byers not only lost the building where his paper was housed, he barely escaped the flood with his life. Water inundated his family's ranch house outside of town, picking it up and depositing it on a small island. An army colonel rescued the Byers family by boat. Byers almost immediately began setting up a new headquarters for his newspaper—but this time he located it on high, dry ground far from Cherry Creek. Soon the newspaper was printing and distributing copies throughout Denver.

Many other townspeople joined Byers and quickly rallied to begin the immense task of cleaning up and rebuilding their city. Because the area of Auraria to the west of Cherry Creek lay lower than the original Denver City to the east, Auraria had suffered more destruction. Owners of businesses that had been ruined in Auraria rebuilt on the east side of Cherry Creek, lessening the rivalry between the east and west sides of Denver. The creek that had once divided the city now united it.

ROCKY MOUNTAIN NATIONAL PARK

THE FIRST RECORDED
ASCENT OF LONGS PEAK

1868

In August 1868 a small group of men gathered at Grand Lake, a small town on the western border of what is now Rocky Mountain National Park. Even though they were brave and determined men, they may have held some secret doubts about what the next several days held for them. After all, they were attempting to make an ascent of Longs Peak, at more than fourteen thousand feet, a towering mass of rock that had already defeated other climbing teams. The daring group included John Wesley Powell; William Byers; Powell's younger brother, Walter; Byers's brother-in-law, Jack Sumner; and three students named Keplinger, Farrell, and Garman.

On horses, the climbers rode away from their base camp on August 20 hoping to climb Longs Peak from the south side. A mule carried a ten-day supply of food for each man. Within two days they had to abandon their horses as they came to what looked like an impassable tangle of chasms and precipices. Keplinger went ahead to scout out a possible route to the summit. He returned believing he had found one.

On August 23 at six in the morning, Powell and his company followed the route Keplinger had mapped out. They soon came to a sheer face of smooth, unbroken granite. There were no trees or shrubs to cling to. No vegetation grew here except for a little gray lichen. Was this the end of their excursion?

At 14,259 feet Longs Peak is the highest mountain in Rocky Mountain National Park. It's been called "America's Matterhorn." This magnificent mountain was first sighted in 1820 by an army expedition led by Major Stephen Long while he was trying to find the source of the Platte River. Major Long's group noted the location of the mountain, but they were some distance away and did not try to climb it.

One of the men in Powell's expedition, William N. Byers, was the founder of Denver's first newspaper, the *Rocky Mountain News,* which he had begun in 1859. He was a powerful force in the Denver area. But Byers was more than an editor. He called himself a "mountain tramp." He enjoyed camping, hiking, and exploring Colorado's mountains and writing about his adventures in his newspaper.

In August of 1864 Byers's wanderings in the mountains had led him into a high mountain valley at about 7,522 feet. He and three friends from Denver had followed the primitive trail of an earlier wanderer in the area, Joel Estes, who first visited this valley on a hunting trip in 1859. Estes thought the area held promise as a cattle ranch, so he came back with his wife and children to settle in 1863.

The Estes trail that Byers and his party followed was so poor that it proved impassable for their wagon. The men cached some of their supplies, loaded the rest on their horses, and rode to the Estes homestead, where they were warmly welcomed as the first visitors seen that year.

Byers and his companions explained that they wanted to climb Longs Peak. Stories had circulated that Ute and Arapaho may have climbed the mountain, including one persistent tale of an Arapaho named Old Man Gun who supposedly climbed to the top of Longs Peak to trap eagles.

With high hopes of being the first to record an ascent, Byers and his group started their climb to the top of Longs Peak on August 19, 1864. Joel Estes's son went along as a guide. But search as hard as they might, they could not find a useable route to reach the summit. They settled for climbing to the top of nearby Mount Meeker, where they added their names to the register there.

After this first attempt Byers wrote: "We are quite sure that no living creature, unless it had wings to fly, was ever upon its summit, and we believe we run no risk in predicting that no man ever will be, though it is barely possible the ascent can be made."

Three years after Byers's unsuccessful attempt to climb Longs Peak, John Wesley Powell arrived in Colorado. Major Powell and his party came from Bloomington, Illinois. First they made a twenty-four hour trip by carriage to Chicago. Next they took the Chicago and Northwestern Railroad to Omaha, Nebraska, and then they took the Union Pacific Railroad to Cheyenne, Wyoming, where they bought horses. They rode the rest of the way to the Denver area.

In 1867 Powell and his party, including his wife, scrambled up Pike's Peak. From this exhilarating perch they could see Longs Peak, 103 miles to the north. It immediately became Powell's new goal to reach its summit.

Powell no doubt knew that there were many differences involved in climbing these two mountains. While Pike's Peak is gently rounded, Longs Peak is a craggy monster with several enormous vertical cliffs barring the way to the top.

Powell was not one to shy away from obstacles. Born in 1834 in New York, he showed an early interest in botany, geology, and zoology. He traveled throughout Wisconsin, Illinois, Iowa, and Missouri collecting shells and minerals, and explored parts of the Mississippi, Ohio, and Illinois Rivers. Powell was an ardent abolitionist. At the outbreak of the Civil War in 1860, he joined the Twentieth Illinois Volunteer Infantry, eventually losing his right arm in the battle of Shiloh. After the wound healed Powell returned to battle and remained in the army until the end of the war.

The one-armed Civil War veteran became a geology professor at Wesleyan University in Illinois. He continued to have a passion for exploration and managed to secure money so that he and his students could spend summers in the field. In 1868, the year after his successful climb up Pike's Peak, Powell made a second visit to Colorado. This time he brought with him thirty students on what was called the Colorado Scientific Exploring Expedition, a trip sponsored by the Illinois State Natural History Society.

William Byers, despite having written that he doubted anyone would successfully climb Longs Peak, was still quick to join Powell and his group when he heard about their attempt to climb the mountain.

And now, even when confronted with a seemingly impassable face of granite, the men were determined to proceed. Almost inch by inch they began climbing the last leg of their ascent. Often their lives depended on finding a small crevice that could be used as a finger-hold. By ten o'clock that morning, the group stood on the summit, having completed the first documented climb of Longs Peak.

In spite of rather fierce winds, Powell, Byers, and the rest of the group stayed at the top of the mountain for about three hours, savoring their successful effort. From the summit they could see Pike's Peak, the Saguache Range to the west, Medicine Bow and Sweetwater Ranges to the north, thirty alpine lakes, Denver, and the plains stretching out in the distance.

The men took barometric and temperature readings and built a monument of small stones. They signed a sheet of paper and put it and their various readings into a tin baking soda can and wedged it into rocks at the top of the peak. They also unfurled a small flag that waved in the breeze. Major Powell gave a short speech before the men left the peak. He celebrated what they had done and predicted still more great accomplishments ahead. This prophecy came true for Powell. Just a short time later, in 1870, he won national fame for his exploration of the Colorado River.

Although the climb up Longs Peak had taken a long time and they were now almost without food, Powell, Byers, and the others spent another cold night out in the open before returning to their base camp at Grand Lake. Byers wasted no time in spreading the news of their first ascent of Longs Peak by publishing an account of the climb in the *Rocky Mountain News* on September 1, 1868.

Reaching the top of majestic Longs Peak was a dream of many mountaineers in the last half of the nineteenth century, a dream not realized until Powell and his group made their successful attempt in 1868.

IDAHO

THE TEST OATH

1885

They were a dozen men, all deputies of the US marshal, and they were on a difficult mission.

They started in the Cache Valley, in the little town of Oxford—in the spring a lush and green oasis but now, in the middle of winter, deeply covered in snow. They were headed not on any road, but instead east, up over the high mountains, the northern reaches of the Wasatch, through thickly snowed-in forests. They did not want their targets to know of their approach.

So deep was the snow that they traveled mostly by bobsled, careening down mountainsides, barely avoiding injury. One of them had brought a thermometer, and they saw the temperature reach thirty degrees below zero. After four days, they had crossed the mountains and were overlooking the Bear Lake Valley. In it, just below them, was the little town of Paris, the county seat of Bear Lake County.

They had been on the move day and night, and as they saw the flickering lights of town below, it was still night. The group stopped, set up camp, carefully started a campfire, and cooked a meal. They rested until just before dawn. Then they headed down the mountainside and strode into town.

The men split up, heading to seven houses in town. They arrested the men in these houses, rousted from sleep in some cases, on charges of illegal cohabitation. Several were sent to jail.

This was only one of a series of raids. Another came at nearby Montpelier, when three deputies arrested several men on similar charges. In that case a crowd of local people gathered, surrounded the deputies, and freed the men, who were never identified.

Some of these arrests later brought convictions, which should not have been surprising. They were convicted not by their peers but by their political adversaries.

The deputies had been sent out by US Marshal Fred T. Dubois, ordinarily a leader in the local Republican Party, but who the year before had organized a new political party called the Anti-Mormon Party. After the election of 1884, it controlled the Idaho legislature and passed a variety of new laws aimed at members of the Church of Jesus Christ of Latter-Day Saints.

Dubois was among the growing number of people at the time who disapproved of the church's teachings allowing polygamy (a provision the church reversed a few years later). Besides that, most church members then were Democrats. Putting the two facts together, the Idaho territorial legislature passed a test oath law, which required voters to swear that they were not members of any church that taught what the Mormon Church taught. For a decade the law kept active Mormons from voting, serving on juries, or holding public office.

The law did not pass easily. When the bill got to the office of the territorial governor, William Bunn, he met with some of its backers, including Dubois, and said he was thinking about vetoing it. One of those men, Jim "Kentucky" Smith, walked up to him, pulled a gun from his pocket, and said, "Governor, you will not leave this room alive unless you sign it and sign it at once." He did.

One of the reasons the anti-Mormons acted so ferociously was that members of Congress had said Idaho would not become a state as long as Mormons had any influence there. With the test oath passed and Dubois's deputies sending to jail anyone who openly said they believed in the church's teachings, the stage was set for statehood. Dubois was elected to Congress in 1886, and three years later he helped push through the bill making Idaho a state. The test oath was repealed a few years after that.

Today, more than a fourth of Idaho's population consists of members of the Mormon Church. Its members have served in all of the state's highest offices.

But remnants of the past remain. Not until 1982 did the state finally, officially, repeal the section of the state constitution—long abandoned as a matter of practice—that kept Mormon Church members from voting or holding public office.

KANSAS

THE POTTAWATOMIE MASSACRE

1856

The year 1856 was a wild one in Kansas.

The territory, newly settled by whites but not yet an official state, had become a battleground over the question of slavery. The 1854 passing of the Kansas-Nebraska Act had repealed the Missouri Compromise of 1820 and allowed for slavery above the 36' 30" line, the latitudinal mark that fell just past Kansas's southern border. Popular sovereignty was to decide whether Kansas—not quite north and not quite south—would be a slave state or a free state. Kansas was brimming with abolitionist settlers; some morally objected to slavery, while others were motivated by their wish to live in an all-white community of homesteaders, rather than a landscape dotted with plantations and blacks. However, the territory was saddled next to the slave state of Missouri, ensuring that Kansas would have a difficult and bloody time carving out its identity.

Zealots on both sides of the fight traveled to Kansas from the north and south to leave their mark; some towns, such as Atchison and Leavenworth, were pro-slavery, while others, such as Lawrence and Topeka, were free-staters. By 1856, skirmishes, town raids, and individual killings over slavery had turned the eyes of the nation on

Kansas. When Governor Wilson Shannon resigned from office that summer, he remarked, "Govern Kansas! . . . You might as well attempt to govern the devil in hell."

This period of "Bleeding Kansas" reached a fever pitch with the destruction of Lawrence, an abolitionist stronghold, on May 21, 1856. It was a piercing victory for the pro-slavery factions; the people and buildings of Lawrence lay dead and burning, and most of the offending "Border Ruffians" from Missouri had escaped unscathed. While the people of Lawrence were still reeling, one man thirsted for vengeance.

John Brown was a New England man, but in 1855 he had joined five of his sons homesteading in Kansas Territory. The men built a log cabin called "Brown's Station" along Pottawatomie Creek, where they hoarded weapons, traded harsh words with their pro-slavery neighbors, and maintained hopes to bring Kansas into the Union as a free state. Brown's sons and their friends, led by John Jr., called themselves the Pottawatomie Rifles.

Upon hearing that Lawrence would be attacked, the Rifles and the elder Brown assembled and began their journey to defend the town. Along the way, they received word that the town already had burned. Brown boiled with indignation over the ease with which the Ruffians had destroyed unsuspecting Lawrence in the early-morning hours. En route to Lawrence, he heard of yet another offense to his cause—the brutal beating of abolitionist US senator Charles Sumner on the Senate floor by a southern congressman, following Sumner's passionate speech entitled "The Crime Against Kansas." By then, Brown was seeing red. While the Pottawatomie Rifles debated what to do next, he had his own plan.

Brown told Rifle member James Townsley, who happened to have a wagon with him, that he'd received news of unrest back at Pottawatomie Creek. Would Townsley take him and his boys back, so that they might keep watch over their home? Townsley agreed, setting out the afternoon of the twenty-third with John Sr. and his sons Frederick, Owen, Watson, and Oliver, as well as Brown's son-in-law and another militiaman. A couple miles from home, the group turned off the road to camp for the night. That evening, John Brown finally made his real plans known. He asked Townsley to take the group several miles up the creek, to the area where he lived, and point out the homes of each pro-slavery man. Then, Brown said, they would make a murderous sweep of all the homes. Townsley refused, suggesting that they fight pro-slavery leaders in open fields at the nearby capital of Lecompton rather than murder men in their own homes. But Brown was undeterred. The next night, May 24, he and his group set out with swords and rifles.

Brown and four others first knocked on the door of the James Doyle residence while Townsley and the rest fought off an attack dog. When Doyle and two of his sons came out of the house, Brown shot the elder Doyle in the forehead. It was the only shot the group would fire, favoring instead the quiet of their swords so as not to alarm neighbors. Brown's two youngest sons stabbed the Doyle sons to death; one managed to get away, dripping blood as he ran, but ultimately was cut down.

Next, they knocked on the door of the Allen Wilkinson residence; Wilkinson was marched south of the house and killed with a short sword by one of Brown's sons.

The band then crossed the Pottawatomie to reach the home of Henry Sherman, known as Dutch Henry, a pro-slavery militant. Dutch Henry wasn't home, though, so Brown's men instead killed his brother, William Sherman, with swords and left him lying in the road.

After midnight, five men were dead. The number would have been higher, had Brown had his way. Several pro-slavery men marked by Brown were not found, including George Wilson, probate judge of Anderson County, who had been attempting to drive free-staters out of the territory. According to Townsley, Brown said "that the Pro-slavery party must be terrified and that it was better that a score of bad men should die than that one man who came here to make Kansas a free State should be driven out."

Brown and his company rejoined John Jr. and the Pottawatomie Rifles the next night; John Jr., presumably unnerved by his father's actions, resigned from his position as captain of the militia and kept watch over the renegade group in his cabin and his brother Jason's cabin. After several days of lying low, the men received word that John Brown was being hunted. The group left on horseback, hiding in forests and strengthening their numbers with more free-staters. John Jr. and Jason stayed behind and were taken prisoner by Henry Pate, a pro-slavery fighter who had participated in the raid on Lawrence.

Hearing of his sons' capture, Brown and his band, now thirty strong, started toward Black Jack Point, where Pate reportedly was camped. When the group neared the camp on June 2, seven men remained with the horses while the rest assailed Pate and his men, quickly cornering them in a ravine and fighting until Pate surrendered three hours later, ultimately freeing Brown's sons. This, the Battle of Black Jack, is considered by many to be the unofficial first battle of the Civil War. Indeed, the entire Bleeding Kansas period—which escalated tensions across the country and killed approximately fifty-five people—set the stage for the war between North and South.

Brown himself kept his finger on the national pulse toward war, spending the years following the Battle of Black Jack devising a massive uprising against the federal government and its slavery-enabling laws. In 1859, he led a siege on the US Armory and Arsenal at Harpers Ferry, Virginia, and attempted to invoke a slave revolt. The mission failed, and Brown was hanged.

His death inspired great sentiment within the anti-slavery movement and made him something of a martyr. In an 1881 speech, scholar and former slave Frederick Douglass delivered a speech at Harper's Ferry, stating, "Did John Brown fail? John Brown began the war that ended American slavery and made this a free Republic." By 1910, however, when former president Theodore Roosevelt gave a speech in Kansas to commemorate a John Brown memorial, leading thinkers such as Roosevelt and William Allen White saw Brown as a misguided extremist. When in 1941 the nationally known Kansas painter John Steuart Curry painted in the state capitol a mural of a wild-faced Brown wielding a Bible and a rifle, much controversy ensued; many Kansans objected to the idea that Brown might represent the people and heart of their state.

EXODUSTERS

1877

Before the town of Nicodemus even existed, pamphlets and posters enticed Lexington, Kentucky, blacks with the claim, "The Largest Colored Colony in America."

In the decade or so since the Civil War's end, southern blacks had endured the trials of Reconstruction, a period in which poverty and racism continued to shackle newly "freed" slaves despite federal occupation of the area. Lacking education, skills, or legal protections to navigate the free world, many continued to work for their old masters as sharecroppers. By 1877, they were willing to leave their longtime home in the South for a place that promised land ownership, cheap living, freedom, and adventure. Western Kansas, a vast swath of prairie grass far beyond the Mississippi River, was just such a place.

The promises came from two men: W. H. Smith, a black minister from Kentucky, and W. R. Hill, a white land developer from Indiana. In 1877 they joined forces on 161 acres of Graham County, population seventy-five, to form the Nicodemus Town Company—named for the legendary slave who purchased his own freedom. Reverend Smith assumed the role of president, and Hill became treasurer. They set out to foster a truly free, all-black community, and make a buck in the process.

The first brave settler, Reverend Simon P. Roundtree, arrived in June, soon followed by Smith's daughter and her husband, Zack Fletcher, who became the secretary of Nicodemus. The town's inception was extremely humble; so few trees were to be found on the western Kansas landscape that the settlers lacked timber for building, and were forced to make their homes in earthen dugouts on the prairie.

This didn't stop Smith and Hill from exaggerating the resources of their new town to black would-be settlers. A wealth of animals to hunt! Horses to be tamed! Land to be homesteaded! The fliers they distributed to southern blacks, mostly in Kentucky and Tennessee, called the area "the Great Solomon Valley" and extolled a rich, fertile landscape quite different from the dry, windswept plain that awaited settlers. But former slaves who were starving and oppressed in war-ravaged states didn't take much convincing. Plus, many associated Kansas with the famous abolitionist John Brown and with its bloody struggle to finally enter the union as a free state.

A black man from Louisiana, S. L. Johnson, wrote a letter to Kansas governor John St. John in 1879 demonstrating the great esteem in which southern blacks held the place. "I am anxious to reach your state," he wrote, "because of the sacredness of her soil washed by the blood of humanitarians for the cause of freedom." (St. John gave a speech welcoming the southern blacks, though he later tempered such comments, perhaps due to political pressure from whites who were wary of Nicodemus and similar settlements.)

Reverend Roundtree and a black carpenter named Singleton helped with the promotion cause, the latter earning the name "Moses of the Colored Exodus" for leading blacks from the south to Nicodemus. In the late summer of 1877, more than three hundred southern black "Exodusters" emerged from the nearest train station, in Ellis, and walked fifty-five miles to their promised land; within weeks came the first birth of a black child in the county to Henry Williams and his wife. Nearly another hundred settlers followed in the next two years.

They weren't entirely thrilled with what they found.

One woman, Willianna Hickman, explained her first impression of the town in 1878:

> *When we got in sight of Nicodemus, the men shouted, "there is Nicodemus!" Being very sick, I hailed this news with gladness. I looked with all the eyes I had. "Where is Nicodemus? I don't see it." My Husband pointed out various smokes coming out of the ground and said, "That is Nicodemus." The families lived in dugouts. . . . The scenery was not at all inviting, and I began to cry.*

People lived "like prairie dogs," she said, digging holes in the earth along the Solomon River for shelter. The dry, flat stretch of tall, yellow grass and limestone earth was a shock to those who had spent their lives in the green, forested hills of the South. Lacking tools, food, planting seeds, and money, some returned to their homes in the South. Others stayed, including Reverend Daniel Hickman and his wife Willianna, of Kentucky, who founded the First Baptist Church in a sod structure.

Their first attempts at growing crops offered little return, owing to the hard ground and difficult climate. During the first hard winter, some black settlers were forced to turn to the Osage Indians for food and assistance.

Nonetheless, through years of hard work, the Exodusters turned their new home into a successful agricultural economy. Favorable weather in the mid-1880s resulted in high yields for their wheat and other crops; amid this prosperity, one county resident, Thomas Johnson, managed to grow his land ownership to one thousand acres.

The mid-1880s boom in Nicodemus spread beyond the fields. Black businessmen thrived alongside white business owners, and stone structures replaced dugout homes. Thirty new buildings went up in 1886. The sod Baptist church was replaced with a stone sanctuary. The Fletcher-Switzer House, constructed in 1880, provided a post office, hotel, stable, and school, all launched primarily by Zack and Jenny Fletcher, the town founder's daughter. They filled the roles of postmaster and postmistress, hotel/stable owner, and schoolteacher. In addition, Jenny helped establish the African Methodist Episcopal Church, which began in an earth structure in 1879 but graduated to a limestone building in 1885.

Soon, Nicodemus was nearly five hundred strong, with a bank, newspaper, drugstore, three general stores, two hotels, and three churches—and miles of fields beyond its commercial center. By the late 1880s, just a decade after its inception, it boasted more stores and churches, pharmacies, barbershops, a second newspaper, an ice-cream parlor, and its own baseball team and band. Resident Edward P. McCabe became the first African American to hold a major state office in Kansas, serving two terms as state auditor, from 1883 to 1887.

The *Nicodemus Cyclone* celebrated the triumphs of former slaves in a June 15, 1886, commentary: "Nicodemus . . . was originally settled by the colored race, and by their patience and untiring energy have succeeded in gaining a grand, glorious victory over nature and the elements, and what used to be the Great American Desert now blooms with waving grain."

Soon, Nicodemus received word that the Missouri Pacific and the Union Pacific railroads might lay tracks through town as they expanded westward. The town approved thousands of dollars in bonds to attract the companies, but both bypassed the town. Union Pacific instead laid tracks six miles away, south of the Solomon River.

This turn of events threatened disaster for Nicodemus, as many businesses talked of making the short move to the railroad to boost business. The *Nicodemus Cyclone* warned against such actions on September 7, 1888:

We are sorry to see several of our business men making preparations to move to the proposed new town. We consider this a very unwise move and one they will regret. With a thickly settled surrounding, already established in business and as reliably informed in the extension on the Stockton road in the near future, Nicodemus and her business men have nothing to cause them alarm. For every one that goes now we will get ten wide awake men next spring. Don't get frightened hold on to your property and be ready to enjoy the real boom that will surely come.

But the businesses moved anyway, establishing a camp south of the river that later would be known as the town of Bogue. Coupled with the economic depression of the 1890s, it was a blow that knocked Nicodemus from its brief period of prosperity. The following decades marked a long decline, as more and more families left their struggling town. The Dust Bowl and Great Depression wreaked further havoc on local agriculture, and by 1935 Nicodemus was down to just seventy-five inhabitants.

Unlike other black settlements west of the Mississippi, though, the town would survive. In 2009, Nicodemus was home to twenty people and was the only remaining town in the West founded by former slaves. Locals and the town's descendants have taken great care to continue to honor the great achievements of Nicodemus's settlers, and the town was named a National Historic Site in 1996.

MISSOURI

THE NEW MADRID EARTHQUAKE

1811-1812

In the early-morning hours of December 16, 1811, the citizens of the little town of New Madrid on the Mississippi River were thrown from their beds. Their houses shook violently, cracks appeared in their brick chimneys, and everything on the shelves cascaded to the floor. Outside in the barns all the animals began to bleat and howl. The residents of New Madrid had woken up to an earthquake.

People fled into the cold night, grabbing whatever clothes they could in the rush to escape their trembling houses. Once they were outside, they huddled together for warmth and security, hoping and praying they would live to see sunrise. Every few minutes there was another tremor, and the terrified pioneers wondered if it would ever stop.

As dawn broke, the ground shook with another great tremor, and the settlers witnessed the ground undulating like waves lapping the shore. Rifts opened up in the earth, belching forth debris and the nauseating smell of sulfur. An even stronger tremor hit at 11:00 a.m.

Despite the fact that few people lived in the area at the time, there were several casualties. One woman was crushed by her falling cabin. A man fell into a hole in the earth and was never seen again. Two more settlers died from shock and exposure. A half dozen Indians drowned when the riverbank sloughed off into the raging Mississippi.

Boatmen on the Mississippi fared even worse. While the land trembled, the river churned like a pot of water shaken back and forth. Boats overturned or smashed against rocks, and untold numbers of boatmen disappeared into the water.

As the day advanced, people saw the full extent of the damage. Their houses lay in ruins, many of their animals were dead or had run off, and most of the trees in the surrounding wilderness had fallen down. Great chasms in the earth impeded the refugees' passage. They found themselves stranded in a surreal wilderness, on a frontier with no roads and miles away from any help.

Nor was that the end of their suffering. As they set up makeshift shelters to get out of the cold or trudged their weary way to St. Louis or other distant towns, they had to endure more quakes and tremors. On January 23 came a full-scale earthquake just as bad as the first, followed by another bad one on February 4, and the worst of them all on February 7. The final quake threw people off their feet while the waters of the Mississippi receded, leaving terrified sailors stuck in the muddy river bottom, desperately struggling to reach shore before the river came back. The earthquake was so strong that it damaged houses in Cincinnati, four hundred miles away, and could even be felt in the nation's capital, a distance of almost eight hundred miles. In St. Louis several stone houses cracked in two.

According to popular folklore the river flowed backward for three days. While this is a bit of an exaggeration, there is an element of truth to the story. When fissures or breaks appeared in the riverbed, they created waterfalls. Sometimes the riverbed upstream ended up being lower than the portion downstream, so sections of the river would flow backward for a short time before the pressure and flow of the water reasserted itself. Just as dangerous to boatmen were the numerous waterspouts, whirlpools, and collapsing riverbanks created by the shaking river. Dozens of boats are known to have sunk, and many more probably slipped unreported into the deep.

The river washed away the following towns: Little Prairie, which became known as the "Lost Village"; an Indian town a few miles south of New Madrid; and New Madrid itself. New Madrid stood on a bend in the river, and the north bank of this bend eroded nearly a mile, taking the old town with it. All but two families moved away from the area, and it would be some time before the new New Madrid would become a town again . . . a mile north of its original location.

A few years later, in 1815, the federal government offered free land to those uprooted by the quake, but most victims had already left the region, and dishonest people claiming to be from the affected area took most of the free land. This swindling of the government became a great controversy, and for many years the term "New Madrid claim" was synonymous with any sort of dishonest dealing.

The rural nature of the region kept the death toll from being higher, but the area is much more populated nowadays. New Madrid currently has a population of more than three thousand. Seismologists still worry about what they call the New Madrid Seismic Zone. In 1990 local residents were treated to two tremors, measuring 4.6 and 3.6 on the Richter scale, a scale ranging from 1 to 10 that scientists use to measure the strength of an earthquake. No one was seriously hurt in those quakes. The New Madrid earthquake of 1811, on the other hand, was probably more than 8 on the Richter scale.

Seismologists hope there will never again be one that bad.

A SLAVE SUES FOR HIS FREEDOM

1846–1856

In April 1846, a slave named Dred Scott walked into a St. Louis court-house and filed suit against his owner, Irene Emerson, claiming he wasn't a slave at all. He also stated that his wife, Harriet, and two daughters, Eliza and Lizzie, were also free. The clerk at the court office must have been astounded. Slaves rarely sued their masters, and the evidence in support of Scott's case was rarer still—it was his life story.

Scott was born a slave in Virginia around 1800. His first master, Peter Blow, moved to St. Louis in 1830 and soon sold Scott to Dr. John Emerson, a US Army surgeon, who took him to Fort Armstrong in Illinois. Illinois was a free state, but Scott was apparently unaware that merely by living there he could claim his freedom.

Dr. Emerson later transferred to Fort Snelling, in what is now Minnesota. This area, then part of the Wisconsin Territory, was also free. Once again Scott appeared unaware of the law, and no one tried to relieve Emerson of his "property."

During his stay in the Wisconsin Territory, Scott married another slave, Harriet Robinson. Her master was a justice of the peace and married the two in a civil ceremony. Marriage was not allowed in slave states, which did not recognize slave marriages as legally binding. Emerson transferred back to St. Louis but hired out his slaves for a time in Fort Snelling, an illegal act in a free territory. The doctor moved again, this time to Louisiana, where he married Eliza Irene Sanford and sent for his slaves.

Soon the group headed back to Fort Snelling, and during the trip Harriet gave birth to the Scotts' first daughter, Eliza. The delivery occurred on the Mississippi River between Illinois and the Wisconsin Territory, both free areas. The group later returned to St. Louis, where Dr. Emerson died.

After his death Dr. Emerson's widow rented out her slaves. In 1846 Scott tried to buy freedom for himself and his family, which soon included a second daughter, Lizzie. Irene Emerson wasn't interested in giving them up, however, and Scott decided to sue.

His suit was funded by the sons of his former master, Peter Blow, who wanted to free the man they used to play with as children. The case appeared strong. Dred Scott had spent considerable time in free areas, his master had broken the law by renting him out in one such area, Scott's marriage to Harriet had been confirmed by a civil ceremony reserved for free people, Harriet had also spent considerable time in free areas, and their first daughter was born in a free area. If they were free, then their second daughter was also free by virtue of being born to free parents. There was even legal precedent—courts in several slave states had liberated slaves who had resided in free areas.

At first Scott was stymied by a technicality. The St. Louis circuit court threw out his case because he had no witnesses to prove Irene Emerson owned him. A new trial eventually began in 1850, and this time the judge ruled in Scott's favor, but Emerson appealed to the state Supreme Court. At this point Scott ran into trouble. Chief Justice William Scott ruled:

> [N]ot only individuals but States have been possessed with
> a dark and fell [malevolent] spirit in relation to slavery,

whose gratification is sought in the pursuit of measures,
whose inevitable consequence must be the overthrow and
destruction of our Government. Under such circumstances,
it does not behoove the State of Missouri to show the least
countenance to any measure which might gratify this
spirit. (Scott vs. Emerson, 15 Mo. 576 [1852], 586)

This decision denied the family's freedom in order to avoid trouble between slave and free states. While it was a political rather than a legal decision, Chief Justice William Scott's prediction proved correct. A civil war was in the offing, and this case would help lead the country into it.

Scott now went to federal court. His tenacity was beginning to draw attention from the press, and he became a *cause célèbre* among abolitionists. Irene Emerson had since moved away and remarried, so now Dred Scott had to fight Irene's brother, John Sanford, who claimed authority over the Scotts.

Scott sued Sanford in the US Circuit Court for wrongful imprisonment, stating that he was forced into slavery. He also sued for nine thousand dollars because Sanford had hit him. Sanford claimed that a black man was not a citizen of Missouri and therefore couldn't sue in federal court, but the court rejected this argument.

The case was heard in May 1854, and the court followed the reasoning of the lower court and ruled that the Scotts were slaves. But Dred Scott had too much at stake to give up. He now headed to the US Supreme Court, which heard the case in February 1856.

At that time the nine Supreme Court justices included three slave owners and two more who came from slave-owning families. The chief justice, Roger Taney, came from a big tobacco-growing family that owned many slaves.

The opinion Taney formulated in the case, which all but two justices agreed with, was a radical one. He ruled that blacks weren't citizens of the United States, despite being state citizens, but decided that his court would hear the case anyway. He even said that blacks were "so far inferior . . . that they had no rights which the white man was bound to respect" (*Dred Scott,* 19 How. 407).

Then Taney stated that the federal government couldn't rule on slavery in the territories, despite the Constitution's provision that "Congress shall have Power to dispose of and make all needful Rules and Regulations respecting the Territory or other Property belonging to the United States." Taney reasoned that this applied only to territories owned when the Constitution was approved in 1787. He furthermore stated that banning slavery, or freeing slaves who went to a free territory, deprived people of their property in violation of the Fifth Amendment. Even the people of a territory couldn't vote to abolish slavery, since it went against the constitutional right to own slaves. Dred Scott would remain a slave.

It was clear to everyone this decision was a political one. Just two days before, President-elect James Buchanan, a staunch supporter of slavery, said the future of slavery needed to be decided by the courts and that he would abide by the result. Many Northerners, especially Republicans, were outraged. A junior politician named Abraham Lincoln claimed that Taney and the Court were conspiring with Buchanan and other Democrats to spread slavery throughout the United States. Indeed, records show Buchanan was kept informed of the case's developments, so he knew which way the ruling would go when he made his speech. Many Northerners feared there would be another case ruling that if slaves were not free even in free states, then slavery was legal everywhere.

In the end, Northern fear surrounding the ramifications of the Dred Scott case helped Lincoln win the 1860 presidential election, leading to the secession of the Southern states and the Civil War.

And Dred Scott? After the ruling the Blow family purchased the Scotts and freed them on May 26, 1857. Sadly, Dred Scott died less than nine months later. He enjoyed his freedom for only a short time, but his tireless fight was a major cause of the war that freed his people.

MONTANA

THE SLAUGHTER OF THE BUFFALO

1883

Of the many species of wildlife that greeted early explorers of the West, the bison made one of the most profound impressions. Even the earliest American settlers were familiar with the animal—commonly known as the buffalo—because its original range extended almost all the way to the Atlantic Ocean. But it wasn't until settlers moved onto the Great Plains that they realized just how prolific the big beast was. Seemingly endless herds blackened the prairie, providing the Indians with everything from food and clothing to shelter and utensils.

Yet, in a surprisingly short time, the buffalo would come perilously close to vanishing from the face of the earth. By the 1830s none could be found east of the Mississippi River, and Josiah Gregg, an early traveler on the Santa Fe Trail, commented that buffalo were "rarely seen within two hundred miles of the frontier."

As early as 1855 the US government tried to protect the buffalo, but it failed miserably. By then the magnificent beast had become a target for every hide hunter, sportsman, and target shooter west of the Mississippi. One of these, an English nobleman named Sir George Gore, killed

2,000 buffalo, 1,600 deer and elk, and 105 bears during a single outing along the Platte and Missouri Rivers in the mid-1850s.

The mass slaughter continued after the Civil War. As Indian tribes unwillingly abandoned their homelands to increasing numbers of farmers, cattlemen, and miners, the buffalo's numbers dwindled. First, the hide hunters, or buffalo runners, decimated the herds roaming the southern plains, taking the hides and leaving the meat to rot in the sun. Then they focused their attention on the northern range.

But hunters feeding a national fancy for buffalo robes were not the only reason for the rapid obliteration of the species. As the army battled to subdue the Indians of the West, the government realized that the extermination of the buffalo could mean an end to the tribes that depended on the beast for their daily subsistence. Officials changed their minds about protecting the animal and instead began to encourage its annihilation.

General Philip Sheridan, commander of the army's Division of the Missouri, was reported to have said in 1875 that

> *The buffalo hunters have done in the last two years and will do more in the next year to settle the vexed Indian question, than the entire regular army has done in the last thirty years. They are destroying the Indian's commissary, and it is a well-known fact that an army losing its base of supplies is placed at a great disadvantage. Send them powder and lead, if you will; for the sake of a lasting peace, let them kill, skin and sell until the buffaloes are exterminated.*

Given this mentality among high government officials, the fate of the American bison was sealed.

When the southern herds were nearly gone, the hide hunters began operating out of Miles City, Montana. Phenomenal herds still grazed on the northern plains. US Marshal X. Biedler of Montana told of traveling in 1879 through a herd that extended for seventy miles!

But the buffalo of the northern plains were doomed to the same fate as their fellows in Texas, Kansas, and Nebraska. By 1883 the Montana and Dakota herds had almost disappeared, and most of the hide hunters had either found new occupations or migrated to Canada to continue their gruesome work there.

In early 1886 William Hornaday, the chief taxidermist at the US National Museum in Washington, DC, went west to look for buffalo specimens for a new exhibit at the Smithsonian Institution. He had heard alarming reports that the bison was extinct, and he decided he could wait no longer. Arriving at Miles City, Hornaday's party started its search immediately. After eight weeks of frantic hunting, the group finally found twenty-five specimens, which were killed and mounted for display. The following year, a party from the American Museum of Natural History traveled to the same area and in three months saw not a single buffalo.

The nation's original buffalo population is officially estimated to have been sixty million animals. Today, after careful management, some three hundred and fifty thousand remain, most of them scattered on preserves such as the National Bison Range south of Montana's Flathead Lake.

THE HARD WINTER

1886-1887

In Montana Mother Nature is never so cruel as in winter, when temperatures can plunge well below zero and snow can reach the rooftops. And no Montana winter in recent history was more cruel than the "Hard Winter of 1886–1887." Never before or since have white inhabitants experienced such extremely cold temperatures for such a long time. As a direct result of that devastating winter, ranchers learned that they couldn't depend on the open range to support their livestock year-round, and they began to provide shelter and food in winter months.

The spring and summer of 1886 were exceptionally hot and dry. As early as May and June, sweltering temperatures were being recorded, and rainfall became so rare that many streams and watering holes dried up. Prairie fires were rampant, burning thousands of acres of the parched grassland. Some sections of the territory had received less than two inches of rain in twelve months.

As the cooler days of fall approached, the open range in Montana supported more cattle than ever before—possibly more than one million animals. What little grass had survived the drought was heavily overgrazed. There were indications that the winter would be severe. Granville

Stuart, the owner of the DHS Ranch, one of the largest in Montana, recalled that many birds that usually wintered on the range disappeared, and the cattle grew unusually thick coats of hair. "Teddy Blue" Abbott, who worked as a cowboy for Stuart at the time, remembered seeing his first arctic owls, which usually lived farther north.

Two weeks of fair weather just before Christmas made the ranchers hopeful, but on Christmas Eve the snow began to fall. By December 27 the Missouri River at Fort Benton had frozen solid, and the weather station at Fort Assiniboine registered a temperature of thirty-seven degrees below zero. Temperatures across the territory hung below zero for days on end. Teddy Blue wrote years later that the Christmas Eve storm lasted sixty continuous days.

On February 3, 1887, the temperature at Fort Assiniboine dropped to 55.4 degrees below zero—the lowest ever recorded there. With the wind chill factor it was ninety-five degrees below zero. Cattle began dying like flies. What little grass remained was frozen beneath several feet of snow, and the hungry livestock cut their feet and legs trying to paw through the icy crust to get at it. As author Joseph Kinsey Howard described it: "Starving cattle staggered through village streets, collapsed and died in dooryards. Five thousand head invaded the outskirts of the newborn city of Great Falls, bawling for food. They snatched up the saplings the proud city had just planted, gorged themselves upon garbage."

Cattle weren't the only ones suffering from the severe cold. The residents of the small towns of Montana were faced with shortages of supplies, especially coal, flour, and wood. By the time the storm ended in March, there was almost no fuel left at Fort Benton. What few supplies were still available commanded exorbitant prices: coal, sixty dollars a ton; flour, seven dollars a sack; and green wood, twenty dollars a cord. Potatoes weren't available at any price.

A person had to be insane to go out in such weather, but the cowboys believed they had no choice. They worked day and night, for weeks on end, trying to rescue what cattle they could from freezing and starvation.

Teddy Blue, in his book *We Pointed Them North*, described what he wore on the range: two pairs of wool socks, a pair of moccasins, a pair of Dutch socks that came to the knees, a pair of overshoes, two suits of heavy underwear, pants, overalls, chaps, a heavy shirt, wool gloves, heavy mittens, a blanket-lined sourdough overcoat, and a sealskin cap. Even with all these clothes, he noted, he didn't stay very warm.

Throughout February the storm raged. Finally, in March, warm chinook winds moderated temperatures. The snow vanished quickly, and thermometers at Fort Assiniboine read forty-six degrees above zero. The ice that had clogged the Missouri River melted, causing floods downstream.

Teddy Blue reported that, of the forty thousand cattle grazing the DHS Ranch in the fall of 1886, including ten thousand newly branded calves, fewer than seven thousand head, including only about one hundred yearlings, were counted the following spring. He estimated that 60 percent of all the cattle in Montana had perished during the winter. Their bloated bodies lay scattered across the countryside.

Many of the large ranches failed as a result of the disastrous winter. Some had been heavily in debt to begin with. The survivors made sure they never put their valuable stock in such a vulnerable position again. The days of the open range were numbered.

GLACIER
NATIONAL PARK

GRINNELL'S SINGLE SHOT

1885

> This is more impressive—stupendously, almost unbelievably beautiful—than any view to be seen in the whole length and breadth of the Alps. And as for Yellowstone Park, compared with this part of the Rockies, it [is] merely flat country!
>
> —*Dr. George Bird Grinnell to James Willard Schultz,*
> *Blackfeet and Buffalo: Memories of Life among the Indians*

It was a glorious fall day in 1885, sunny and crisp, and James Willard "Apikuni" Schultz was leaning back on a tree, his hat pulled down over his eyes. It felt good to let the warm sun seep into his bones—he knew it was one of the last chances he had to feel truly toasty until the next spring. Many winters spent in northern Montana had taught him to catch the warmth and try to store it, bringing it out again on those days when the sun didn't shine and the mercury dipped below zero. Again.

Eventually he heard the creaks and groans of the mail stage coming down the road; he stood up and brushed the dust and leaves from his pants and settled his hat on his head. A man descended from the stagecoach, fit and trim and of medium height, in well-worn clothes much like his own. He was Dr. George B. Grinnell, conservationist and editor of *Forest and Stream* magazine, and he hoisted a canvas-covered bedroll, a war sack, a Sharps .45-caliber rifle, and a fly rod as he strode over to Schultz. Schultz grinned: This was not the bookworm editor or Washington bureaucrat he had placed bets would appear. Relieved, they made their introductions, saddled up, and headed off for one of the most historic forays into Glacier Park that any writer or conservationist ever made.

A few mornings later, Schultz and Grinnell were joined by Yellow Fish, who was the son of a man who worked for the American Fur Company and a Pikuni woman, and they set out with a team of horses and a wagon to make camp in the St. Mary Lake country. Grinnell had come to Montana to document the area, hunt, and then return to Washington with animal trophies for the Smithsonian, and he was eager to get into the wild. The going was tough because they were attempting to pull the wagon over a game trail and had to stop frequently to cut aspen trees to widen the path. Nonetheless, they eventually got their wagon into the flats that separated the upper and lower lakes and made camp a few hundred yards below the upper lake.

On the second day of the expedition, the men went hunting. The day before they had climbed Flat Top, aptly named by Schultz in 1893 for its long, flat expanse, and Grinnell had shot a mountain goat, but the meat had been "too tough and musky flavored to eat," according to Schultz in his book *Blackfeet and Buffalo: Memories of Life among the Indians.* With stomachs rumbling, they were more determined to find meat they could eat and decided to begin their hunt on the mountain just to the south of Flat Top. Climbing up the slope and following game trails, they saw plenty of signs of deer, elk, and grizzlies but no other big game. Schultz wrote:

> *We had not gone far when, a couple of hundred yards*
> *ahead of us, a lone bighorn ram bounced out from a*

depression in the shale and went leaping swiftly on; at a distance of about three hundred yards he stopped, turned sidewise and stared at us, head proudly up, his perfectly circled horns, like washtubs, carried as though they had no weight at all. No more had it stopped than Grinnell brought his heavy rifle to his shoulder, quickly sighted it, fired, and the ram made one high leap, plowed down into the shale, and was still.

It isn't easy work to butcher an animal on a mountain and haul the meat back to camp, but the three hungry men did the job willingly. Later that evening, while the trio feasted on broiled fat ribs, they relived the finer points of the day, as men around campfires have done throughout the ages. Relishing the shot that found its mark even at such a tremendous distance, Yellow Fish cried out, "Oh, *ho, hai!* . . . he did not kneel and rest his gun; just stood and aimed it, and with one shot killed the very far-off bighead." And so they named the mountain Singleshot, in honor of the shot that saved them from going to bed hungry for the second night in a row.

That episode marked the beginning of Grinnell's influence on the naming of many of Glacier's most notable features. Sometimes the names were chosen for obvious reasons, as was the case with Goat Mountain, where Grinnell, Schultz, and Yellow Fish encountered an abundance of mountain goats, and Mount Citadel, which was so dubbed for its spired summit. In other cases they chose names based on people they wanted to honor, as is the case with Grinnell Lake, Grinnell Glacier, Grinnell Mountain (these three were named by Schultz, not Grinnell), Little Chief Mountain (the Pawnee nickname for Grinnell's friend, Captain Frank North), Almost-a-Dog Mountain (a Pikuni friend of theirs), and Reynolds Mountain (Grinnell's assistant editor at *Forest and Stream*). And with a nod to his very first hunting trip at Glacier, Grinnell and the other members of his party named Fusillade

Mountain for a hunting expedition in which a reported twenty-seven shots were fired at a band of goats, yet not a single animal was struck.

Grinnell and Schultz had become acquainted through a professional relationship. Schultz was a contributor to *Forest and Stream*. In the winter of 1883–84, Schultz asked Grinnell to use whatever clout he had in Washington to help save the Pikuni Indians. In his book *Signposts of Adventure: Glacier National Park as the Indians Know It*, Schultz reported that during the previous winter, the buffalo herds had been exterminated and the tribe had had to rely upon the populations of antelope, elk, deer, rabbits, and grouse on their reservation, but by fall even those were gone, and the tribe began to starve. It took months for Grinnell to accomplish much, due to the red tape in Washington and the slowness of travel, but in February Grinnell's wagonloads of food finally arrived.

This was only one of many times Grinnell advocated for the tribes. He was well known and well liked among the Indians he met, and they honored him by naming him, just as he honored the land he loved by naming what he found. He was called Gray Clothes by the Gros Ventre, Fisher Hat by the Blackfeet, White Wolf by the Pawnee, and "wikis," which means bird, by the Cheyenne, who noted that his comings and goings in the area were like a seasonal migration.

Grinnell's affinity for all things wild seems to have begun at birth, when he was given the middle name Bird. As a youngster he attended school at John James Audubon's home in New York and continued his studies at Yale, where his academic record left something to be desired but his passion to be a naturalist was unmatched. He went on his first dinosaur dig in 1870 and then served as the expedition naturalist for General George Custer on his trip to the Black Hills in 1874. These trips resulted in Grinnell's continued study of paleontology, and in 1880 he earned a doctorate in the field. Shortly thereafter, he assumed the editor position at *Forest and Stream*, the leading publication at the time for sportsmen and naturalists. He used the magazine as a forum for exploring the problem of diminishing game populations and disappearing habitat, thus sparking a national awareness about nonrenewable natural resources. He also devised the notion of the game-warden system that was financed by small, equal fees from all hunters and managed by the states. This was a radical departure from the undisputed and unregulated right to hunt that had reigned over the country until that time. One enthusiastic reader of *Forest and Stream* was Theodore Roosevelt, who worked with Grinnell to end what they saw as federal neglect of Yellowstone Park, as well as excessive commercialization there. Grinnell's conservation philosophy was the foundation Roosevelt used to build the American approach to conservation.

Grinnell's interest in the park was not simply to hunt there and bring specimens back to the Smithsonian in Washington, DC, although he took that role seriously. Nor was he there simply as an anthropologist performing an academic exercise, meeting Indians and living somewhat as they did. Grinnell, perhaps foreseeing days when the nation would boom and expand in all directions, wanted to preserve this incredible corner of the earth for the animals he so admired. Of all the things Grinnell did to shape our nation's natural heritage, perhaps the finest was this: He was one of the three commissioners to sign the treaty with the Pikuni in 1896, acquiring the mountainous part of their reservation, which later became the remarkable corner of the earth known as Glacier National Park.

NEBRASKA

HOMESTEADING

1863

Daniel Freeman pounded on the door to the land office. It was just after midnight on January 1, 1863. Freeman, a Union soldier, had slipped up to Brownville, Nebraska, from his post at Fort Leavenworth, Kansas, with one thing on his mind. He wanted land.

Freeman raised his fist to knock on the door again when suddenly it opened from the inside. A man stood in the doorway holding a lantern in one hand. He peered out into the night at Freeman.

"Yes? Can I help you?" he said. Freeman's summons at the front door of the land office had clearly roused the man from sleep, as his hair was standing on end and his long nightgown was rumpled.

"I am sorry to have awakened you, sir," began Freeman, "but I am here to apply for my free land."

The land agent shook his head. "The Homestead Act does not become law until January 1. That's tomorrow." He moved to shut the door. Freeman quickly wedged his boot in the door and held up his pocket watch.

"Sir, it *is* tomorrow."

The land agent squinted at the pocket watch then looked at Freeman again. "Well, if you are that anxious to have your land you can come on in, I guess." He backed up and opened the door fully.

Freeman nodded his thanks and followed the man into the land office. He could see an open door to the rear of the main room that obviously led to the land agent's private quarters. He caught sight of a corner of a rumpled blanket with a ceramic chamber pot peeking out from underneath the bed.

The land agent set his lantern down on a polished wooden desk in the middle of the main room. He muttered to himself as he sorted through scraps of papers.

"Aha! Here is it," said the man. He handed the sheet over to Freeman and passed him a quill.

By the soft light of the lantern, Freeman scanned through the document in his hands. For a twelve-dollar fee, he would receive 160 acres of fertile land of his choosing in the Nebraska Territory. This was the result of the Homestead Act Congress had passed the previous year, which President Abraham Lincoln had signed into law. The premise of the Homestead Act was to modernize the West and reduce poverty and overcrowding in the big cities of the East. Lincoln also wanted to establish more free states to help with his desire to end slavery in the United States.

Besides the small fee, the land was free to anyone over twenty-one, male or female, including freed slaves and immigrants. The only catch was the citizen had five years to cultivate the land and build a structure on it. At the end of that five-year period, the citizen would receive a title to the land free and clear.

Freeman had already picked out a site near a small Nebraska settlement called Beatrice, about sixty miles to the west of Brownville. The land he was interested in was near the freight road and a source of running water, Cub Creek. Freeman thought it would be just about perfect.

With a flourish of the quill, Freeman signed his claim. It was ten minutes after midnight on January 1, 1863. Freeman had just become the first person to apply for land under the nation's Homestead Act.

From that point on, more than 270 million acres were given away in thirty states over the next hundred-plus years. Although the Homestead Act was repealed in 1976, Alaska continued the program until the mid-1980s.

During its run, 10 percent of US land was distributed through the Homestead Act. However, only 40 percent of those who applied stayed on their land for the requisite five years. Of the other 60 percent, most gave up due to adverse conditions, such as blizzards, drought, grasshopper invasions, or simply the lack of knowledge to work the land.

The Homestead Act is often praised as being one of the first legislative actions that was equal to both men and women and to both whites and blacks. In fact, the Homestead Act became effective the same day as Lincoln's famed Emancipation Proclamation. However, the act did not provide for Native Americans; in fact, by 1900, 95 percent of American Indian land was lost to homesteading and other land action.

Even though Daniel Freeman applied for his claim in 1863, he had to wait two more years to move to Nebraska and start his new life. In 1865, Freeman finished his military service and started west to his new homestead in Nebraska. Along the way, he picked up his new bride, Agnes. Freeman and Agnes had become engaged via a series of letters written between the two during the Civil War. Agnes had originally been engaged to Freeman's brother who was killed in action.

Freeman knew immediately he had made an excellent choice when he surveyed his property near Beatrice. Cub Creek ran full and fresh and the freight road from town was very close. Freeman got to work clearing the land of its native tall grasses and planted crops using an iron plow. He raised corn, wheat, and oats, along with growing a small orchard of apple and peach trees.

Even though Nebraska was mostly a treeless prairie, Freeman found there were a few trees growing on the banks of Cub Creek. He felled these trees for his log cabin and other wooden outbuildings and used the scraps of lumber as fuel.

One thing Freeman learned about life on the plains was how to make a fence when you didn't have fence materials. Freeman planted a row of Osage orange trees and trained the young shoots to grow horizontal to the ground. By doing so, Freeman could weave the branches together to form a living fence. The process took many years to complete, but, as Freeman found out, Osage orange was such a hard wood and made such a solid fence that it was worth it.

In addition to the crops tended by Freeman, he raised hogs, chickens, and horses. He also relied on his previous medical training and served as a physician for the citizens of Beatrice. Eventually the log cabin gave way to a two-story brick house. Freeman also built a school outside of Beatrice, which was in use until the 1960s.

In 1868, five years after Freeman filed his claim under the Homestead Act, he received the title to his land as promised. Freeman died in 1908 and is buried on his property, now a national landmark to honor and remember those pioneers who helped grow America under the Homestead Act.

ORPHAN TRAIN

1899

By the time the Davis twins boarded the train that would take them out of New York City and somewhere west, they had been orphaned two years. Lena and Anna were twelve years old that summer. They had been found selling matches and newspapers on the streets of New York City, trying to survive. The police, instead of arresting Lena and Anna for loitering, took them to the New York Foundling Hospital and recommended they be placed on an orphan train.

Lena and Anna Davis knew they were lucky to be with the New York Foundling Hospital and its sister organization, the Children's Aid Society. They had heard tales of other orphans living on the streets of New York and forming gangs. Often, those children turned to crime and were arrested and placed in jail alongside hardened adult criminals. The prison system was not safe and was becoming overcrowded.

Since the 1850s, the Children's Aid Society and New York Foundling Hospital had been a haven for orphaned, abused, and neglected children. Those children were cleaned up and given a set of new clothes, then loaded on a special train. The train took them out of New York

City and to states west. Adults waiting for the train would select one or two children to adopt into their family. The children were given a fresh start and a new life.

The train carrying Lena and Anna was scheduled to stop in Nebraska. Lena and Anna had been scared about leaving New York City, the only home they had ever known. They had come to America from Sweden when they were babies, but since their parents died two years before, they had been alone. Lena and Anna didn't even know where Nebraska was when they boarded the train!

The train ride west was uneventful. The Davis twins were careful not to make a mess of their new clothes; they had been told that the people waiting for the orphan train would appreciate nice-looking children.

The majority of the children on the orphan trains were white Christians, and no sick or disabled children were allowed. Even though the train carrying Lena and Anna was a normal train, some orphan trains were specially equipped to carry babies. These trains were fitted with quieter wheels and no whistles, and made frequent stops for diaper cloths and fresh milk.

Lena and Anna were jolted awake one morning after about a week on the train. Looking out the window, they spied a sign stating, WELCOME TO GREELEY, NEBRASKA. The train slowed to a halt as it arrived at the small station. Lena and Anna joined the other children waiting on the platform.

A local minister stepped forward and welcomed the children to Greeley. As he moved to the side, the children could see a crowd of adults watching them. Lena nudged Anna in the ribs and they both stood up straighter.

One by one, the adults came forward and looked over the children. One man, whom Lena judged to be a farmer, walked up to a boy about Lena's age and felt his arm muscles through his new shirt. They talked quietly for a minute and then the farmer approached the minister with the boy at his side.

"Excuse me, Reverend," the farmer said. "I'll take this boy. He says his name is Walter. He looks like he'd be a good help to me on the farm."

The minister smiled and nodded, making a note on a piece of paper he held. The farmer and Walter walked to a waiting wagon.

Lena looked up as an older woman approached her. The woman looked her up and down and then glanced over at Anna.

"Are you two twins, then?" the lady asked.

Lena nodded, afraid to speak. She had heard rumors that even though siblings often wanted to stay together, they usually ended up separating and were adopted by different families. The lucky ones were able to at least live in the same town, but Lena had heard of one set of five children who went to five different villages in three different states! She and Anna didn't want to be separated.

As if she knew what Lena was thinking, the lady smiled and put out her hands to both Lena and Anna. "I could use both of you, if you'd like," she said. "I have baby twins at home and I'd like some help in caring for them."

Lena and Anna exchanged hopeful glances. Could they really stay together? Anna spoke first, turning to the lady. "If you please, ma'am, we'd be happy to join your family," she said.

The lady smiled again and turned to the minister. Soon it was all settled. As Lena and Anna were led to a nearby wagon, Lena turned and looked back at the orphan train. There were other children walking away with their new parents, but those who hadn't been chosen were slowly climbing back on the train. They would get off at the next station and be put on display again.

The Davis twins were lucky in their experience with the orphan train. They ended up in a family that loved them, and within the year, their new parents legally adopted both girls. Some members of the orphan train were not so lucky; there are tales of abuse and neglect by the new parents and some children ran away from their new homes and tried to find their way back to New York City.

From the 1850s to the 1920s, an estimated two hundred thousand children were placed on orphan trains and sent throughout the Midwest and Plains states. Most were grateful for the chance to make a better life for themselves and overcame whatever hardships they had lived with in their childhood. These children were given a future.

NEVADA

BUILDING THE TRANSCONTINENTAL RAILROAD

1868

Building the transcontinental railroad was one of the most ambitious projects of its time. Promoters were eager to build a link from the East Coast to the West to speed the transportation of goods and people from one coast to the other. The army also expected to take advantage of a transcontinental railroad, which would make transportation of soldiers and supplies much cheaper and faster. President Abraham Lincoln signed the Pacific Railroad Act in 1862, authorizing building such a railroad.

The Union Pacific Railroad started laying track from east to west, while the Central Pacific Railroad ran track from Sacramento, California, going east. The most difficult obstacle was the Sierra Nevada. It took crews more time to build the track over these mountains than the entire rest of the route. Eventually the track reached the border of Nevada in the spring of 1868.

The track crossed the Nevada border from Truckee, California, to Reno, Nevada. At that point, the tracks stretched 167 miles from the coast. From there the new track would be laid approximately along the route of today's modern Interstate 80. Engineer Joseph Graham led the charge through Nevada. The first train arrived in Reno from Sacramento on June 18.

Now the race was on. Charles Crocker, one of the financiers of the Central Pacific Railroad, challenged the crews to lay one mile of track per day in a race with the Union Pacific to lay the most track in the least amount of time. His partner Collis P. Huntington urged the crews to work even faster and to take shortcuts when possible, even if it meant going up steeper grades or using wood instead of stone.

Crocker wanted to oblige but he was short of supplies. It took six months for rolling stock and rails to be shipped around South America's Cape Horn and only slightly less time when shipped through the Isthmus of Panama. Often he would have plenty of ties but no rails, or vice versa. The Truckee mills worked around the clock to supply enough ties and cut timber for bridges and trestles.

He was also short of labor. He did not have the advantage of hiring returning Civil War veterans that the Union Pacific did. Those men that did come west preferred working in the mines or in farming. He ultimately hired large numbers of Chinese laborers for the job.

By July 1, crews had laid track to what would become the town of Wadsworth. Graham established this town, which would become a supply base for the railroad builders. The town had an engine house and station buildings, too.

From this point on, the track layers, or "rusteaters" as they were sometimes known, would be challenged by the lack of trees and the lack of water. There was nothing but sagebrush, sand, and white alkali deposits. High mountains rose to the south while barren hills stood at the north. Additional crews had to haul water all the way from the Truckee River to the track layers. Each train that took supplies to the railhead carried vats filled with water to supply railroad water towers. Another crew transferred the vats from the rail cars to wagons to transport them to the crews. They also brought trees from the Sierra Nevada to be used for railroad ties and railroad bridges.

At least the crews would not be faced with staggering mountains. Most of the land was relatively flat. In a 275-mile section, the track only gained one thousand feet in elevation. Crews started making good progress. In July and August, crews spiked forty-six miles of iron, an average of about a mile and a half a day. The Indians in this area did not harass the crews or get in their way, like their counterparts in the Plains states did with the Union Pacific crews. In comparison, the Nevada tribes were docile and mostly stood by and watched the railroad being built.

Every day began at sunrise and started with feeding the livestock. Foremen shouted out orders to the laborers. A locomotive hauled rail cars with the day's supplies out to the end of the line. The Chinese used a gauge and a leveling rod to lay ties to ready them for rails. Then rail gangs loaded the rails from the rail cars onto wagons. Another gang placed the rails on ties. Two men grasped the front of the rail and dragged it out of the car. Several pairs of men then grabbed the rail from each side. When they reached the spot for the rail to be laid, they dropped it in place. The whole process took about thirty seconds per rail.

After the rail was in place, another crew placed the fish plates and drove the spikes, ten to the rail. One more pair of men adjusted and bolted the fish plates. Meanwhile another crew hitched the empty car to a horse team and dragged it back to the base camp for more rails. The process was repeated until the crews broke for meal time at midday. Mobile kitchens provided meals for the crews around noon and at the end of the day.

Far ahead, surveying parties and grading crews prepared the road bed. A Chinese grading crew supervised by an American foreman prepared about one hundred miles of road at a time. They used picks and shovels to remove earth and hauled it away with horse- and mule-drawn wagons. They used black powder and occasionally nitroglycerin to remove rock or build tunnels. Behind them other crews built bridges, culverts, and trestles ahead of the track layers. Still others positioned the ties needed for the foundation for each rail.

Alongside the track layers, another crew erected poles for the telegraph. Each day, an operator sent telegraphs reporting the train's progress to Sacramento. Sometimes they ran out of wood for poles, so the crews had to be innovative. They often used ties, sagebrush, barrels, and other items to keep the wire off the ground. Another crew strung the wire to the insulators on the poles.

To support the crews, blacksmiths repaired tools and shod horses. A harness shop supplied collars, traces, and other equipment for the livestock. The railroad also provided tents for workers and clerks who kept track of accounts and records. Crocker also took care to keep out the gamblers and prostitutes. He did this by charging them an exorbitant amount to water their horses, since water was so scarce. The Chinese didn't really notice their absence since they didn't drink and they gambled only among themselves.

After some initial apprehension by construction superintendent J. H. Strobridge, the Chinese proved themselves to be able workers. They learned quickly, didn't fight, and rarely had strikes. They took nightly baths and had clean habits. They also boiled water for tea, which had the secondary benefit of killing bacteria in the available water. Many other workers who drank from streams and runoff got sick. A type of headman organized each group of twelve to twenty Chinese, collecting wages, purchasing supplies, and sending back money owed to their Cantonese contractors. This person also acted as cook, since the Chinese had their own fish- and vegetable-laden diet.

The only difficulty grew out of a Chinese superstition. They had been hearing talk of large snakes and twenty-five-foot-tall Indians. Ultimately the track bosses sent twenty-two Chinese ahead to see for themselves that the tales were false. When they were satisfied, the work continued.

By October, the line stretched all the way to Winnemucca. The town, named for the old Paiute chief, became a thriving railroad town. By the end of 1868, these crews had laid 362 miles of road. This was approximately the one mile per day promised by Crocker.

In January 1869, the crews reached Elko and continued on to Humboldt Wells. From there the track went northeast toward the state line with Utah. At Humboldt Wells, work progressed more slowly when the temperature temporarily dipped to negative eighteen degrees Fahrenheit. The cold spell lasted a week and froze the ground two feet deep. Graders could not use a pick and shovel, but had to use black powder instead. The weather eventually got warmer and turned the track into a quagmire. Trains had a difficult time passing over it. Some could move only about as fast as an oxcart.

The Central Pacific still had difficulty getting supplies. A serious snowstorm in the Sierras stalled supplies for a while. One train uncoupled in the middle while running down a slope into Reno. The two halves collided, splintering eleven cars and killing two brakemen.

On February 16, the line stretched to a point twenty miles east of Wells. At the same time, the Union Pacific was twenty miles east of Ogden, Utah. By February 29, the line reached a spot forty miles east of Wells, 144 miles from their final destination, Promontory Summit north of the Great Salt Lake in northern Utah. The Union Pacific was sixty-six miles from the eastern side of the point.

From that point on, both sides made a mad dash to reach the meeting point first. On April 28, Crocker accepted a bet to build ten miles in one day. By lunch break at 1:30 that day, the crew had built six miles. At 7:00 p.m. that night, the crews hammered in the last spike, finishing ten miles and fifty-six feet!

Though building the road across Nevada brought its own unique challenges, they were nothing that couldn't be overcome. The Chinese workers proved equal to the task. After taking four years to build the railroad across the Sierra Nevada, they spanned the whole state of Nevada in barely a year. Without their hard work, the railroad would never have been built. When East met West at Promontory Summit in Utah on May 10, 1869, it was a day to be remembered forever.

ABSALOM LEHMAN
DISCOVERS A CAVE

1885

Absalom Lehman bought property in eastern Nevada in the mid-1800s. He built his ranch along a creek that flowed off nearby Wheeler Peak, the second-highest peak in Nevada. One day in the spring of 1885, Lehman noticed a strange depression on the property that piqued his curiosity. He started digging around it and found that the hole grew much larger below the surface. When the hole was big enough to crawl through, he squirmed through it. His eyes widened at the delightful surprise below him. He had just discovered a world of beautiful stalactites and stalagmites! The cave system would later be named for him.

A legend connected with the discovery of the cave claims that Lehman was exploring on horseback, when the horse suddenly broke through a weak spot in the cave's roof. Before plunging to the bottom, Lehman lassoed a tree and held on until he was rescued four days later. According to the legend his legs were permanently disfigured from hanging onto the horse all that time.

How did Lehman come to be there? Lehman left Pennsylvania and traveled to California during the Gold Rush days, but he did not find much gold. He traveled to Australia to prospect, and there he married his first wife. After she died in 1861, he came back to the United States. He remarried in Denver and in 1869, he and his wife, Olive, moved to Nevada. They built a ranch, planted an orchard, and sold food to nearby mining camps. Due to health problems, Olive had to leave the area in 1881, taking their two children with her. It was after he returned from visiting her that Lehman was poking around on his property and made the great discovery. He only carried a candle lantern, but it gave off enough light to illuminate the remarkable limestone cave.

Lehman probably did not realize that thousands of years of chemical reactions had formed the cave. If he had, he might have been able to help prevent later damage to the cave. The limestone beneath Wheeler Peak had been carved by ordinary water mixed with carbon dioxide, which dissolved the rock, leaving hollow spaces and scalloped walls. Later the water drained out of the cave, and then water percolated into the cave from the surface. This water contained dissolved calcite, which created the various formations inside the cave.

Lehman may not have realized the scientific significance of what he had found, but he immediately recognized the moneymaking potential. He started charging people one dollar each to enter the cave. Unfortunately, some formations were destroyed to create paths through the cave. He also hung ropes and erected ladders to assist visitors with navigating the cave. Some areas could only be reached by crawling, but the sights were worth the inconvenience. People were dazzled by the unusual formations inside the cave. By September of 1885, eight hundred people had seen the cave. Hundreds of people visited the cave in the years after that.

The limestone cave was about a quarter of a mile long and was situated approximately 6,800 feet above sea level on the flank of Wheeler Peak. The familiar stalactites and stalagmites were everywhere. A unique formation, called a shield, was common in this cave. One fantastic shield, called the Parachute, had a generally round shape with stalactites hanging from it.

For a while Lehman made quite a profit allowing people to visit the cave. He decided to sell his ranch so that he could live near the cave. But before the sale could go through, he died in Salt Lake City, on October 11, 1891.

The Rhodes family, nearby neighbors, bought some property near the cave from the estate and promoted the cave until it was taken over by the government. On January 24, 1922, President Warren G. Harding set aside the caves as Lehman Caves National Monument. In 1923, the caves became part of a State Recreation Ground and Game Refuge. Clarence and Bea Rhodes were appointed custodians of the caves. They collected fees and gave guided tours. They made some improvements by replacing rope ladders with stairways and excavating floors to make more headroom. They developed one large room to be used as a meeting place where weddings were often performed. Visitors played music on the stalactites and stalagmites, resulting in lasting damage. They improved the roads to the cave entrance and erected overnight tents. They arranged dances, picnics, and pageants on the grounds and built fifteen new cabins and a lodge house. Mr. and Mrs. Elroy Cue took over from the Rhodes in 1930. Shortly afterward, White Pine County bought the property and donated it to the federal government.

The US Forest Service administered the caves until June 10, 1933, when all national monuments became part of the National Park Service. Over the next ten years, the Works Progress Administration, Civilian Conservation Corps, and Civil Work Administration completed several cleanup and rehabilitation projects in and near the cave. A new cave entrance tunnel was completed in 1939 and electricity was installed in 1941. During the 1950s, a visitor center, picnic area, and other improvements were made.

When the federal government established Great Basin National Park as America's forty-ninth national park on October 27, 1986, the Lehman Caves became part of the park. The main attraction today is the Gothic Palace, which is filled with columns, draperies, and stalactites.

The Lake Room is also impressive with tranquil pools and "soda straws," which are hollow limestone tubes through which water is still dripping. The Grand Palace contains shields, massive columns, and "bacon rind" draperies. The formations continue to grow at the rate of one inch every one hundred years. They will continue to grow as long as water continues to seep into the cave. If you look closely, you may also see cave dwellers such as pack rats and cave crickets. Fortunately all this natural wonder is now protected from further carelessness and vandalism.

LAS VEGAS

MORMONS ARRIVE IN LAS VEGAS

1855

William Bringhurst stopped to wipe the beads of sweat that dripped from his forehead and gathered on the back of his bright red neck. The scorching June sun had taken a heavy physical and emotional toll on him and his twenty-nine men. For the past thirty-five days they had pulled, dragged, and pushed forty ox-drawn wagons, fifteen cows, and a few horses through some of the harshest rocks ever assembled into a mountain range. Still, having received a mandate from their leader Brigham Young, the men braved the more than one-hundred-degree temperatures to settle the valley that would eventually be called Las Vegas.

The corners of Bringhurst's mouth formed a wide grin as he looked out over the vision that opened before him. Sharp rocky cliffs had been replaced with lush green fields and fresh running water. Bringhurst and his companions may have looked over the valley that lay before them and rightly wondered if it was simply a mirage created by the desert heat, or if they had found a paradise in the desert. The men quickened their pace and even the animals seemed a bit more spry as the group approached a creek of fresh clear running water. The vision hadn't been a mirage. They had finally arrived at their destination, a valley of green swaying grass and sprouting trees that the Spanish had named The Meadows. Their journey had come to an end and now they could start the work they had come here to do.

It's strange to think that a city built on vices would have its roots in religion, but such is the case with Las Vegas. The thirty men who arrived in the valley on June 14, 1855, were members of the Church of Jesus Christ of Latter-Day Saints (LDS), known as Mormons. The group, led by Bringhurst, had been sent to the area by Brigham Young, the leader of the LDS Church, to protect both the mail and the pioneers who were making their way west.

Almost since their founding in 1820, the Mormons had a difficult relationship with the US government. It all began when their founder and first prophet Joseph Smith claimed to have spoken with God himself and to have translated golden plates he received from an angel. Certainly there were those in government positions who found these claims to be a bit of a threat to their power structure.

Whether or not the claims of Joseph Smith were true, they served as a catalyst that put the fledgling church in direct controversy with members of local government. In fact, the church seemed to gather enemies almost as quickly as it gathered converts. Mayors turned to governors, who themselves turned to the United States to help rid their communities of the pesky Mormons.

While the LDS Church started in New York State, persecution forced its members to keep heading west in search of a place where they could practice their religious beliefs in peace. Government policies (the governor of Missouri signed an order to exterminate them) and mobs pushed them out of Ohio, Missouri, and eventually Illinois. In the winter of 1846, after the murder of their beloved prophet Joseph Smith two years earlier, Young started them on a migration to what would eventually become the state of Utah.

It took the LDS pioneers more than a year to make the trip through the rugged Rocky Mountains, paving trails as they went and doing so largely with handcarts. The trail they created became a major trading and travel route known as the Mormon Trail. In July 1847, Young looked over the valley of the Great Salt Lake and declared it to be "the" place. He claimed most of the Great Basin, including an area that would eventually become part of the state of Nevada. Young petitioned the US government to name his newly formed territory Deseret, but the United States rejected his proposed name and instead named the territory Utah after the Native American Utes who inhabited the region. The naming showed that although the LDS Church had largely escaped oppression, it had not escaped its uneasy relationship with the United States.

Young set up a community, establishing a city he named Salt Lake. But Young's vision for the area did not stop in the Salt Lake valley. He continued to send groups of pioneers west, settling all areas possible in the Utah Territory, eventually reaching all the way to California. Young knew that water was an essential element for survival and so he sent out groups to settle mainly where water was plentiful. He also knew the church and its members couldn't survive without a steady flow of income, and he had an idea.

Communication in the 1800s was done mainly in the form of letters and packages that were given to wagon trains as they went westward. But a new form of transportation had taken hold of the west, making it much easier to get mail. Letters were placed in saddlebags that were then carried by small, fast-moving horses across the plains to the west. Called the Pony Express, the service was looking to expand to California and Young wanted that passage to go through the trail his members had created.

The US government awarded a contract to the Mormons for carrying the mail westward to California. When the United States allocated funds to build a military road on the Mormon Trail, Young took advantage of the opportunity and sent Bringhurst to establish a settlement post in Las Vegas.

Young chose the valley for several reasons. It was almost exactly halfway between Salt Lake and San Bernardino. The Spanish had named the area Las Vegas, "The Meadows," because the valley had an abundance of free-flowing water and lush green grass. Young presumed the area could be easily irrigated, making it easy to grow crops. The area was already an established resting place for tribes of Native American Paiutes and traders.

Having quenched their thirst and that of their animals, Bringhurst and his men searched for a place to build a structure they could use as a fort. The valley was still unsettled, and while the Native Americans were reported to be peaceful, the Bringhurst party feared the possibility of attack from Mexican nationals who still roamed the area. Bringhurst chose a hilltop located a short distance from the springs. The hilltop was flat enough to sustain a structure and the spot allowed the group to foresee any approaching attackers. The thirty men drove their oxen to the hill and unloaded supplies from the wagons, including the material they needed to build the fort. While building the fort was the priority, Bringhurst also intended to contact the Native American Paiutes, teach them how to raise crops, and bring them the word of God.

Bringhurst sent men out to find large stones that could be used as the foundation of the fort. As the stones were found, they were brought up the hill on wagons and laid out. With the fort underway, Bringhurst established relations with the Paiutes: "We agreed to treat them well and they were to observe the same conduct towards us." Bringhurst appointed George W. Bean, who spoke the Paiutes' language, as a translator. Bean worked well with the Paiutes and through his conversations with them learned how to make bricks of sun-dried mud, called adobe. The bricks were used to build the walls of the fort. Bean reported back to Young that "the [Paiutes] were soon partially converted to habits of industry and helped us grub the land, make adobes, attend the mason, and especially to herd the stock."

When the 150-square-foot fort was complete, it had walls that stood 14 feet high with bastions positioned on the northwest and southeast corners. The men also cleared mesquite trees, planted crops, and built cabins with wood from the nearby mountains. While the fort had an encouraging beginning, it was doomed almost from the start. The soil in the area was extremely alkaline and even though water was plentiful, the men found it impossible to grow crops. They were also unaccustomed to the searing heat that baked the valley. In fact, the heat was one of the main reasons the Paiutes did not have a constant presence in the area. The group had also chosen possibly the worst time to settle, arriving at the beginning of the hottest time of the year. What few crops the settlers did manage to grow were almost completely destroyed by the unencumbered sun. One settler wrote: "The prospect for the land looks slim. Most of the wheat is badly blasted."

The Paiutes themselves did not help the quickly dwindling situation. They didn't see any problem with freely taking the white man's crops for their own needs and did so on a regular basis. By the time the first winter arrived, all but seventeen of the settlers had returned to Salt Lake. Bean remained and one day while talking with the Paiutes discovered that they knew of lead deposits in nearby Mount Potosi. Bean reported the find to Brigham Young, who sent Nathaniel V. Jones to the mine to determine if the ore could be removed and shipped to Salt Lake. Jones arrived at Mount Potosi and began the work of mining the ore.

As the ore came from the ground, Jones ordered his miners to mold the lead, but found it "very hard to smelt." The frustrated Jones tried over and over again to pour lead into molds but every time the molds were opened, the lead cracked. Unfortunately, what the inexperienced Jones didn't realize was that he was not working with pure lead, but a mixture of lead and silver. Not realizing that they had been mining a precious metal, Young ordered them to abandon the mine in January 1857, leaving the discovery of silver for other settlers.

Young "realized the spirit of the mission was broken," according to Bean, and made the decision to abandon the fort. In February 1857, Young wrote a letter authorizing the brethren to return to Salt Lake. "Although some remained behind, the last of the settlers finally left the valley when the Paiutes took the remaining crop." While the fort may have been unsuccessful, the road the Mormons established remained a major travel route to California. The remains of the fort were eventually purchased by the State of Nevada, which operates it as a museum. The LDS Church eventually returned to Las Vegas and grew in membership, building a temple in 1989.

NEW MEXICO

SHOWDOWN IN LAS VEGAS

1880

It was January 1880, and the weather had turned cold in the vicinity of Las Vegas, New Mexico. Late in the month, four cowboys—Tom Henry, John Dorsey, James West, and William Randall—rode into the small village, intent on warming themselves with some good whiskey. While they were there, they decided they might as well gamble a little and treat themselves to some female companionship. By the time long shadows stretched across the dry prairie that surrounded Las Vegas, the four visitors were drunk and making nuisances of themselves.

Local law officials attempted to reason with the four men, politely asking them to turn in their weapons until they were ready to leave town. The cowboys flatly refused to part with their revolvers. For a while the sheriff did not force the issue, hoping the situation would resolve itself. But finally, after several days of hard drinking had turned the four cowboys into real troublemakers, Sheriff Joe Carson made his move.

On the evening of January 22, Carson confronted the four men at the Close and Patterson dance hall in East Las Vegas. This newer—and wilder—part of town had sprung up with the arrival of the railroad the previous year. The men were still drunk, and this time Carson insisted that they disarm while in town. They refused again, cursing and laughing derisively. As Carson backed away from the foursome, one of them pulled a pistol and fired. Carson drew one of his two pistols and shot twice. By this time all the drunken cowboys were shooting, and Carson fell to the floor. In the meantime Carson's deputy, David Mather, opened fire on the rowdies. When the shooting stopped, Carson and Randall lay dead, and West was writhing with the pain of a gunshot wound to his stomach. Observers reported that nearly forty rounds had been fired in less than one minute.

Dorsey, unscathed, and Henry, limping because of a gunshot wound in the leg, took off for the Lewelling and Olds Corral. They stole two horses and quickly left town. West was carted off to jail. Mather covered Carson's body and sent a bystander up the street to fetch the undertaker.

Two days later the local newspaper, the *Optic,* shed more light on the incident:

> *Today we visited Mrs. Carson, who is heart-broken and
> disconsolate over the brutal murder of her husband. She
> has his garments, which are perforated with bullet holes,
> carefully folded away in her trunk. There are eight bullet
> holes in his coat, and one in his boot, showing that he was
> shot nine times. . . . On the night he met his death, Joe
> had two revolvers on his person, one in a scabbard around
> his body and one in his hip pocket. The chambers in the
> latter one were empty and, as traces of blood are visible, it
> is thought that poor Joe managed to get it out of his pocket
> and fire two shots at his assailants.*

A couple of weeks after the shootout, the two men who had escaped, Henry and Dorsey, were sighted several miles away in Mora County. A posse rode off toward the tiny village of Mora, nestled in the mountains some thirty miles to the north.

Surprisingly the two fugitives surrendered peacefully to the posse. On February 6, residents of Las Vegas gathered around the jail as the murderers were led to their awaiting cells. The mob questioned the posse members about whether the captives had shown any remorse, but all they could learn was that the prisoners blamed the entire unfortunate affair on "whiskey."

Henry and Dorsey did not have long to think about their fates. On their second night in the county jail, they and West were yanked out of their cells by a crowd of angry citizens and marched to the windmill that stood in the middle of the plaza in West Las Vegas. Nooses were placed around the three men's necks, and they were asked if they had any last words. Someone gave the signal and tightened the ropes. The first of the killers, West, dropped from the platform of the windmill and, as the crowd watched, his body swung back and forth in the slight winter's breeze.

But Sheriff Carson's widow thought hanging was too good for these outlaws. She stepped from the crowd and started firing a rifle into the bodies of her husband's killers. The rest of the spectators joined in and, when the shooting stopped, all three desperadoes were dead, their limp bodies riddled with bullets.

A coroner's jury was convened to investigate the deaths. Its verdict was clear and straightforward. It found no wrongdoing on the part of Mrs. Carson or any other citizen. It did find that Henry and Dorsey "came to death by several shots in their heads," and that West displayed "signs of being hanged by the neck by some person or persons unknown." The verdict ended with the statement, "We also found that the doors of the jail were broken open and from investigation we learn that the above men [the killers] were taken out of their cells by a mob, unknown to this jury."

Miguel A. Otero, New Mexico's territorial governor from 1897 to 1906, once wrote:

For more than a year after the entry of the railroad, it can be stated without fear of contradiction that Las Vegas was the "hottest" town in the country. Such a statement would be substantiated by the record, for one month, which . . . old files . . . establish. They show that twenty-nine men were killed in and around Las Vegas, either murdered outright or shot in self-defense or hung by the well-regulated Vigilance Committee. Such a record, I am certain, would be hard to parallel in the history of any of the wild towns of the West.

THE DEATH OF BILLY THE KID

1881

Billy the Kid felt exhausted as he bedded down in Pete Maxwell's house in Fort Sumner, New Mexico. It was mid-July 1881, and the slightly built, bucktoothed boy, who sometimes went by the name Henry Antrim and other times called himself Henry McCarty, was on the run again. This time he was trying to evade Sheriff Pat Garrett, who was on his trail for escaping from a makeshift jail in the Lincoln County Courthouse on April 28. During the breakout, the Kid had killed two men, deputies Robert Olinger and James W. Bell.

The Kid had already been found guilty of murder in Mesilla, New Mexico, on April 13. There, Judge Warren H. Bristol of the Third Judicial District had ordered him to be held in Lincoln until May 13, 1881, when he was to be "hanged by the neck until his body be dead." He had spent only a week in the Lincoln jail before escaping.

On the day of the escape, Sheriff Garrett had been out of town collecting taxes. He had left Olinger and Bell in charge of the Kid and several other prisoners. Around noon Olinger assembled the prisoners to take them across the street to the Wortley Hotel for lunch. The Kid asked permission to go to the privy behind the courthouse. While

Olinger escorted the other prisoners to lunch, Billy reportedly recovered a pistol that someone had left for him in the outhouse and killed Bell.

The Kid watched out the second-floor window of the courthouse, armed with Olinger's own double-barreled shotgun, as the deputy scampered back across the street at the sound of gunfire. The courthouse custodian, Godfrey Gauss, yelled at Olinger that the Kid had just killed Bell. Just then Olinger saw Billy in the upstairs window aiming the shotgun at him. "Yes, and he's killed me too," were reportedly Olinger's last words before Billy dropped him in a pool of blood.

About an hour after the killings, Billy the Kid mounted up and left Lincoln for the last time. He met with no resistance from any of the townspeople, causing Sheriff Garrett to remark later that:

> *The inhabitants of the whole town of Lincoln appeared to be terror-stricken. The Kid, it is my firm belief, could have ridden up and down the plaza until dark without a shot having been fired at him, nor an attempt made to arrest him. A little sympathy might have actuated some of them, but most of the people were, doubtless, paralyzed with fear when it was whispered that the dreaded desperado, the Kid, was at liberty and had slain his guards.*

One of Billy's legs was still in shackles when he left Lincoln on a stolen horse. He stopped at a friend's ranch nearby and removed the cuff. Then he made a fateful decision. Instead of heading south into Mexico, where he could escape the posse that he knew would soon follow him, he chose to ride to Fort Sumner, a town he knew well. The Kid's poor judgment and perhaps a lack of appreciation for Sheriff Garrett's tenacity proved to be his undoing.

After several weeks of searching for the Kid, Garrett learned that he was in Fort Sumner. Finding it hard to believe that Billy would return to a town in which he was so well known, Garrett decided to check out the information anyway. With two deputies he rode to Fort Sumner, arriving on the night of July 14, 1881. When the three lawmen pulled up in front of Pete Maxwell's house, Garrett told his men to wait outside while he interviewed Maxwell. Garrett disappeared into the house.

Soon afterward the Kid stepped onto the porch on his way to the meat house to retrieve a beefsteak for supper. Since neither of Garrett's deputies had ever seen either the Kid or Maxwell, they had no reason to suspect this man who strolled across the porch in his stocking feet. One of the deputies, John W. Poe, assumed that "the man approaching was either Maxwell or some guest who might have been staying there." He went on to describe what happened next:

> *He came on until he was almost within an arm's length of where I sat, before he saw me, as I was partially concealed from his view by the post of the gate. Upon his seeing me, he covered me with his six-shooter as quick as lightning, sprang onto the porch, calling out in Spanish, ";Quién es?" (Who is it?)—at the same time backing away from me toward the door through which Garrett only a few seconds before had passed, repeating his query, "Who is it?" in Spanish several times.*

The Kid bolted back inside. Garrett, catching the Kid's silhouette in the moonlight, drew his revolver and shot twice. Billy the Kid fell dead to the floor.

The following day Garrett wrote to the governor of New Mexico Territory, Lionel A. Sheldon, to tell him that Billy had died from a gunshot wound that "struck him in the left breast and pierced his heart." A coroner's jury cleared Garrett of any wrongdoing and further stated that "we are united in opinion that the gratitude of all the community is due to said Garrett for his action, and that he deserves to be compensated."

The name of no other outlaw in American history may be as widely recognized as that of Billy the Kid. Yet some of his past is still shrouded in mystery. The best indications are that he was born in New York City in 1859, the son of Patrick and Catherine Devine McCarty. After Patrick died around 1864, Catherine and her children moved to Wichita, Kansas, and in 1873 to Santa Fe, New Mexico, where she married William H. Antrim. It was in New Mexico that the Kid picked up his most common alias, William Bonney.

So much has been written over the past one hundred years about Billy the Kid that it is possible for one to draw just about any conclusion about the youth's short life. Garrett acknowledged that Billy "was open-handed, generous-hearted, frank, and manly." But other more recent writers have not been so kind. One historian, Jeff Dykes, once called the Kid "that mythical hero, the Robin Hood of the Southwest, who was once just a buck-toothed, thieving, murderous, little cowboy-gone-bad."

Whether Billy was a "little cowboy-gone-bad" or whether he was rotten from the start is a question that will be debated for as long as the olden days of the American West are discussed and studied. One thing is certain, however. Garrett shot and killed an American legend at Pete Maxwell's house on the night of July 14, 1881.

OKLAHOMA

AFTER THE TEARS

1846

The story of the Cherokee Trail of Tears has been told many times, and rightly so: It was one of the most important, and shameful, episodes in all of American history. Yet the story does not end there. What happened to the surviving Cherokees after they reached their destination? Was there life after the Trail of Tears? That story is less well known, and it provides an inspiring counterpoint to the tragedy of Indian removal, a new chapter marked by resilience and endurance.

The losses on the Trail of Tears had been terrible almost beyond imagining. At least fifteen hundred people had died in the stockades in Georgia while waiting to depart. Another sixteen hundred or more had perished during the journey due to hunger, disease, and exposure. Successive waves of exiles arrived at the new Cherokee lands in the West during 1838 and 1839. Some required two months to cover the eight hundred miles, while others took as long as four months because of the harsh conditions. More people died in the months immediately after arrival, struck by disease and shorted on rations by corrupt government contractors.

Those first months were among the hardest that the Cherokees had to face in their new territory. To survive, they were forced to fall back on some of their ancestral ways. Supplies were so scarce that many did not have bowls and pots or simple utensils with which to eat. In their previous existence back east, these items were available for sale or barter at stores and trading posts; but now most Cherokees were so poor that they had no money and nothing to trade. Tribal elders remembered how to make clay pots for cooking and holding water. They carved spoons out of wood, and made shoes and clothing out of animal hides. In addition, the government had confiscated their firearms, so for a time the Cherokees had to employ bows and arrows for hunting in order to put meat on the table.

There were many other adjustments that had to be made in order to adapt to their new home. Soils and climate were different from what they were accustomed to. Many of the best parcels of land were already taken by earlier Cherokee emigrants, and the 1839 newcomers had to make do with more marginal areas. Some found it difficult to adapt and sought solace in alcohol, or resorted to crime. But most struggled on and worked constantly to rebuild their lives.

Unfortunately, one aspect of Cherokee society that survived the Trail of Tears intact was the old tribal animosities. The recriminations over the removal treaty continued for years to come, the tribe still split between those who had opposed the treaty and those who had consented. Several prominent signers of the treaty, including Elias Boudinot and John Ridge, were assassinated as traitors by members of the anti-treaty John Ross faction. The Treaty party mobilized for revenge, with a view of ultimately overthrowing Ross as chief of the Cherokees. Many of the so-called Old Settlers, who had preceded the other two groups to the West, also resented John Ross and his rule.

It took all of Ross's political skills to try to reconcile these differences and bring some semblance of unity and stability back to Cherokee life. A milestone in this effort was the Treaty of 1846, in which the

Ross party agreed finally to accept the terms of the 1835 removal treaty that they had reviled, and to share the federal payment for their former lands among all factions of the tribe. Amnesty was also granted to Treaty party renegades, who now agreed to accept Ross's leadership. Ross saw the 1846 treaty as an assertion of Cherokee independence and national unity. For ordinary Cherokees, it meant they would finally receive their long-delayed and much-needed compensation for removal.

Such money was important to the continuing struggle to rebuild the Cherokees' economy and social fabric. By the 1850s, they had made remarkable progress in this direction. The Cherokee population, according to best estimates, was about 14,000 in 1851 (still down from 16,500 in 1835); by 1860, the number had risen to 22,000. A public school system was established with more than two dozen schools. Seminaries for both men and women were created for the training of teachers, with professors drawn from the best universities in the East. In Tahlequah, the capital of the Cherokee Nation, there were government buildings including a supreme court, five hotels, numerous law offices, stores, and a brick Masonic temple. A bilingual newspaper, the *Cherokee Advocate,* was also published in Tahlequah. In nearby Park Hill, one could see the fine residences and carriages of the half-blood Cherokee elite. Throughout the Cherokee Nation, there were similar signs of social and economic advancement—dozens of blacksmith shops, sawmills, and gristmills, and cattle, hogs, and horses in the tens of thousands. Steamboats ran up and down the Arkansas, carrying cotton and other trade goods to the Mississippi and the larger world beyond.

Yet the unity and stability of the Cherokee Nation was always fragile at best, and tragically, in establishing their new nation, the Cherokees made the same mistake as America's founding fathers. They accommodated a great social and political evil, slavery, which ultimately would tear their nation apart once again, just as it shattered the Union. African American slaves had helped their Cherokee owners survive on the Trail of Tears, and slave labor underlay much of the prosperity that had since come to the Nation. Lewis Ross, for example, the well-to-do brother of Chief John Ross, arranged for five hundred slaves to be shipped to Indian Territory in 1838. Subsequently, on his own lands, 150 slaves operated valuable salt works when they weren't engaged in raising crops for export. Despite the obvious importance of slaves to the Cherokee economy, harsh codes were enacted that prohibited them from attending school, learning to read, or walking anywhere without a pass. By 1860 there were about four thousand slaves in the Cherokee Nation, but only 10 percent of Cherokees were slave owners, causing another sharp division in their society. "The traveler, passing through the Cherokee Nation," wrote explorer Josiah Gregg in 1844, "is struck with the contrast between an occasional stately dwelling, with an extensive farm attached, and the miserable hovels of the indigent . . . with a little patch of corn." Combined with the longstanding divide between full-bloods and half-bloods, and the old division between the Ross party and the Treaty party, the issues of slavery and secession split the Nation asunder in 1861. Siding with the Confederacy, the Cherokee government made a poor bargain.

Much of what the Cherokees had built since 1839 was laid to waste over the next four years of the Civil War. Their population was decimated, as they were hit hard by disease, starvation, and marauding guerrillas. John Ross himself was captured by Union troops in 1862 and spirited out of the territory. A large number of slaves escaped in the chaos, and some went north to join the First Kansas Colored Infantry, which distinguished itself at Honey Springs (July 17, 1863), where they fought their former masters in the battle that decisively broke Confederate control over much of Indian Territory. When the war was over, the Cherokees, along with the other nations of the so-called Five Civilized Tribes, were punished more severely than any former Confederate state. What would the Cherokee people do now?

They began to rebuild their society once more—this time, without slavery.

BOOMER SOONER

1890

It is somehow appropriate that the first mayor of Oklahoma City was killed in a dispute over land. In some sense he brought it on himself. William L. Couch had been a leader of the Boomer movement, which for years had agitated to open the lands of the Indian Territory to settlement. By the time President Harrison finally approved an opening in 1889, the Boomers' promotions had brought land hunger to a feverish pitch. There were far more claimants than there were good claims to go around, and fights became inevitable. As the fatal bullet crashed through his kneecap, the irony was probably lost on Couch.

The Boomers had actually been a rather peaceable lot. Since 1879, first under David L. Payne and later under Couch, they had pursued a kind of civil disobedience in the territory. By the dozens and sometimes by the hundreds, they would go where they were forbidden and begin building cabins, clearing trees, and busting sod. Then soldiers of the US Army would appear, round them up, and escort them to the Kansas border. Couch had personally led six of these invasions. The Boomers never expected to stay. Instead, they sought to establish a principle—one that hardly needed to be established, that this was a "white man's country"—and to raise consciousness. They held meetings, published a newspaper, and mailed out flyers, promoting Oklahoma across the nation as a new Promised Land.

A later generation might call what the Boomers did "hype," but their hype worked only too well. On April 22, 1889, as many as fifty thousand people crowded up to the borders of the Unassigned Lands, north, south, east, and west. There were approximately four home seekers for each available plot. It truly was a race for land. Of course, some people hoped to improve on the odds, especially those like Couch and the Boomers who felt some sense of entitlement. Some flagrantly staked their claims well ahead of the big day, while others took jobs with the Santa Fe Railroad in order to be at a convenient location when the starting guns went off. Still others, depending on their means and connections, also found a way into the territory before noontime. There were reports of some suspiciously well-coiffed "deputy marshals" hovering near town sites. Most "sooners," however, just lay in the weeds, awaiting the signal.

Oklahoma City was not entirely a blank slate when noon struck on its day of destiny, but it was close. Then known as Oklahoma Station, it featured only a railroad depot and a scattering of shacks, tents, and pens. When the great moment came, an eyewitness at the station, perched atop a boxcar, recalled that people seemed to materialize out of nowhere, scurrying in all directions, dragging luggage and tools. Within twenty minutes after twelve o'clock, at least forty new tents had been raised in the immediate vicinity. At about a quarter past one, the first apparently legitimate claim seekers arrived on the scene, looking around agape, their horses puffing.

Couch and various members of his family were among those well-placed employees of the Santa Fe Railroad who strolled from the tracks over to their claims sometime near noon. Couch had previously picked out his plot just west of the depot itself, a full 160-acre homestead soon to become famous. As the day progressed, seven more individuals also claimed the same parcel as a farm homestead, while almost six hundred others demanded it be divided into town lots, because of its proximity to the railroad depot. Couch and his rival farm claimants, who had each staked out their own portions of the quarter-section and begun building houses, warned off all such comers, declaring that the land was not part of Oklahoma City. But in time the town lot seekers became insistent enough that for several months army soldiers were stationed on the disputed property to keep the peace. The lot seekers organized themselves and, Boomer-like, invaded the homestead repeatedly, trying to establish a foothold. Again, the irony of the situation was probably wasted on Couch.

Couch had bigger concerns—namely his immediate neighbors who had carved up the land he had so carefully chosen. Couch had resigned as mayor of Oklahoma City after only six months in order to "prove-up" his residence on the homestead, as required by law. He, his wife, and their five children lived in a small house on the property and put in a wheat field. They remained at a standoff with most of their fellow claimants, but from the beginning their relations were hostile with a man named John C. Adams. Among other incidents, Adams had chased one of Couch's sons off his tract with a club, and on another occasion he shot and killed the family dog. Matters reached a crisis on April 4, 1890, when Adams chopped down part of a fence that Couch had constructed to keep Adams's horses out of his wheat. When Couch and one of his sons attempted to repair the fence, Adams came after them with a club, which Couch jerked away from him. Adams pulled out a revolver, but Couch drew his weapon faster, telling Adams to drop it. Couch's son picked up the gun, and he and his father retreated toward their house. Adams, meanwhile, had gone into his own home and emerged with a rifle. Shots were exchanged, and Couch was hit in the left knee.

The wound became infected, and Couch died two weeks later. Adams stood trial for murder and was sentenced to seven years in prison.

There was a final irony that was most certainly lost on Couch: his funeral occurred on the first anniversary of the land run.

The dispute over the homestead next turned to legal channels. Of the seven rivals, the claims of the late Couch and several others were disallowed by the General Land Office because they were shown to be "sooners." The battle now boiled down to two individuals, John Dawson and Robert Higgins, a doctor from Kansas. Dawson strove to show that Higgins was also guilty of "soonerism," because he had crossed the starting line on April 22, 1889, to water his horses. Higgins contended that he had done so, but that he had witnesses to show that he had returned to his place and run the race legitimately. The case took five years to settle and went all the way up to the US secretary of the interior, who decided in Dr. Higgins's favor.

Higgins gave the widow Couch twenty-one lots from the land her husband had once claimed. Most of the thousands of legal disputes that erupted out of the 1889 Land Run did not end so magnanimously. The opening of the lands had been symbolic of the frontier myth in which Americans so fervently believed, and when the Promised Land failed to be delivered to them, they did something that was also quintessentially American—they called on their lawyers.

OREGON

THE GREAT MIGRATION

1843

On a fine autumn day in the late 1830s, Philip Leget Edwards, a young Missouri man, surveyed the beautiful Willamette River Valley from his vantage point in the mountains. For nine months he had endured remarkable hardships, toiling across the Great Plains and the Rocky Mountains before arriving in Oregon. Now, as the birds sang and flitted about him, he enjoyed this paradise at the end of his long trail.

A small spiral of smoke to the north signaled the location of the Methodist mission built a few years earlier by the Reverend Jason Lee. And there were a few scattered farms belonging to other Americans who had already made their homes here. Solomon Smith and Calvin Tibbs were among the first whites to settle in Oregon, in 1832. By now, about two hundred others resided in the valley.

Several years later, Edwards wrote of his emotions that day as he viewed the valley he described as "picturesque and lovely beyond anything to which we of the Mississippi valley have ever been accustomed." In a letter to a friend who had inquired about conditions in Oregon, Edwards wrote in the poetic language of the day:

Never shall I forget the wild ecstasy of one hour in that
Territory. . . . I thought of the green phantomland beyond,
whither retires the spirit of the fierce warrior when the
conflict of life is over—and there was intensity of contrast!
Below my feet was all that was soft, and bland, and
holy—and beyond, all was the stern rivalry of sublimity
and grandeur!—and I thought too, of the vast Infinite that
made them all! I know not how long I paused—I started
at the admonition of my solitary Indian guide, brushed
away the unconscious tear from my eye, and rushed down
the dark glen before me—the scene of enchantment was
gone—but the recollection never!

By the early 1840s, Oregon was on the minds of thousands of Americans intent on making the long trip west and beginning a new life in this place so gloriously described by Edwards and other visitors. Already, the two-thousand-mile-long Oregon Trail had been blazed. In 1843, the largest party of settlers to date set out overland to the Pacific Northwest. Their journey would become known as the Great Migration.

Peter Burnett, a Tennessee-born, Missouri-raised lawyer who later was elected the first American governor of California, was the leader of this massive movement. In later years he would identify the force that drove him—and no doubt many other settlers—to Oregon. "I saw that a great American community would grow up, in the space of a few years, upon the shores of the distant Pacific," he wrote, "and I felt an ardent desire to aid in this most important enterprise." Burnett's wagon train to Oregon was typical of those that followed in the next several years. When the party left Independence, Missouri, on May 22, 1843, it comprised nearly three hundred men, women, and children, along with fifty wagons. By the time the train reached the neighborhood of today's city of Topeka, Kansas, these numbers had more than doubled. One hundred and forty-seven days and almost seventeen hundred miles after setting out, Burnett's party reached Fort Walla Walla. Part of the group floated down the Columbia River to Fort Vancouver, while the rest traveled overland to The Dalles and then switched to boats for the final leg of the trip.

Burnett's group, as well as many that followed, found a friend in Dr. John McLoughlin, chief factor of the Hudson's Bay Company post at Fort Vancouver. Prices for commodities were high in Oregon. Burnett wrote:

> [P]ork was ten and flour four cents a pound, and other provisions in proportion. These were high prices considering our scanty means and extra appetites. Had it not been for the generous kindness of the gentlemen in charge of the business of the Hudson's Bay Company, we should have suffered much greater privations.

Burnett estimated that the arrival of his wagon train doubled the population of Oregon. And that was only the beginning. By the time the Civil War broke out in the East, more than a quarter of a million emigrants had left home to seek their fortunes at the end of the Oregon Trail.

By 1848, Oregon had grown so much that it was officially designated a territory. In 1859, it became the nation's thirty-third state.

MAKING HEADLINES
OREGON-STYLE

1846

On a cold Thursday in February 1846, W. G. T'Vault left his office in Oregon City carrying a sizable stack of newspapers—the first ever published on the West Coast. Formerly a lawyer, T'Vault had forsaken the profession to edit the newly founded *Oregon Spectator* for three hundred dollars a year. He was also president of the Oregon Printing Association, publisher of the bimonthly paper.

Oregon City had been home to an earlier newspaper of sorts, the colorful *Flumgudgeon Gazette and Bumble Bee Budget*. Handwritten, it had mostly spoofed local citizens and events rather than reported hard news. Consequently, the *Spectator* is recognized not only as Oregon's first newspaper, but as the first on the entire West Coast of the United States. It predated the first paper in California by six months and the first in Washington by six and a half years. In fact, among western states, only New Mexico, Oklahoma, and Texas beat Oregon to the printing press.

The first issue of the *Spectator* was a single sheet of paper measuring eleven and a half by seventeen inches, folded down the middle to create four pages. It was printed on a handpress that the Oregon Printing Association had ordered from New York. In addition to carrying the text of the Organic Laws of Oregon, which had been proposed by the Legislative Committee of Oregon Territory, the premier issue contained tidbits of homey advice such as the following, printed on page one:

> *Be honest, frugal, plain—seek content and happiness at home—be industrious and persevering; and our word for it, if you are in debt you will soon get out of it; if your circumstances are now embarrassed, they will soon become easy, no matter who may be the editor, or what may be the price of flour.*

Oregon's second newspaper, the *Oregon City Free Press*, debuted on April 8, 1848. Its editor was George L. Curry, a former editor of the *Spectator* and future governor of the state.

News of the California Gold Rush had a deleterious effect on both the fledgling *Free Press* and the elder *Spectator*. Both had to suspend publication temporarily for reasons later explained in an apologetic editorial.

> *The Spectator after a temporary sickness greets its patrons and hopes to serve them faithfully. . . . That "gold fever" which has swept about 3,000 of the officers, lawyers, physicians, farmers, and mechanics of Oregon into the mines of California, took away our printer also.*

A unique feature of early Oregon newspapers was their acrimonious "Oregon style" of reporting. According to Robert F. Karolevitz, author of *Newspapering in the Old West*, the so-called Oregon style was the "forerunner of a free-swinging brand of personal journalism" laced with "vituperative, no-holds-barred editorials."

By the mid-1850s, Oregon boasted three prominent newspapers, all of whose editors were masters of Oregon-style reporting. Thomas Jefferson Dryer of Portland's *Weekly Oregonian,* Asahel Bush of Salem's *Oregon Statesman,* and W. L. Adams of the *Oregon Argus* (the successor to the *Spectator* in Oregon City) all used the pages of their newspapers to denounce each other's politics with, as Karolevitz put it, "a seething cauldron of editorial invective which left their readers gasping."

On one occasion Bush, a Democrat, responded to a printed attack by Dryer, a Whig, by refusing to "get down to the depths he has sunk to . . . for we will not sully our columns with vulgarity and slang." Later, the outraged Bush added:

> *There is not a brothel in the land that would not have felt itself disgraced by the presence of the* Oregonian *of week before last. It was a complete tissue of gross profanity, obscenity, falsehood, and meanness. And yet it was but little below the standard of that characterless sheet.*

One by one, newspapers were established in other Oregon towns. By 1867, Eugene had its *Guard* and residents of Roseburg could subscribe to the new *Ensign* for a mere three dollars a year, paid in advance.

Professional journalism had come to Oregon, and as shaky as its early foundations were, it provided the basis upon which state newspapering traditions of today are built.

SOUTH DAKOTA

TODD THE LOBBYIST
Dakota Territory Is Established

1861

The wagon train was loaded with enough supplies for several weeks. The young town of Yankton was in a flurry of excitement as they prepared to send off their founder, John Blair Smith Todd. Yankton's own young and ambitious lawyer loaded into one of the wagons and settled in for a long and dusty ride east. His journey would take him through Minnesota and Nebraska territories, and on his return trip, he would travel through the Dakota Territory.

Todd had served in the US Army for nearly twenty years before returning to Yankton, the town he had founded. He set up a well-respected law office and enjoyed a fulfilling career. But the hardworking retired army officer desired more. As settlers ventured into the areas around Yankton and points farther west, Todd and his fellow citizens were looking for answers and assistance to drought, conflicts with Native Americans, and the toils of life on the frontier. Additionally, when Minnesota became a state, most of the lands east of the Missouri

River fell into disarray because the US government couldn't administer the massive geographic area.

The Yankton Treaty took much of the land that had been granted to the Lakota tribe and gave it to the US government. The settlers in the areas that became present-day North Dakota, South Dakota, Wyoming, and Montana were left on their own, with a minimal provisional government. Many of them lobbied for territory status but were continually denied. But a certain lawyer from Yankton had an inside angle—he was cousin-in-law to president-elect Abraham Lincoln. So the young lawyer traveled to Washington, DC, on behalf of the citizens of his hometown.

Lobbying for territory status was not easy, as the country was gripping for the Civil War. Asking the government to create a territory nearly the size of New England was a stretch, but by using a blend of his strong-willed army skills and his negotiating ability as a lawyer, Todd was able to lobby the United States Congress and his cousin-in-law to create the Dakota Territory on March 2, 1861.

The lands of the new Dakota Territory included the area north of Nebraska Territory, west of Minnesota Territory and the present western border of Wyoming, north to the Canadian border, and west along the Continental Divide in Montana. Because of its establishment as a trading post and central location, Yankton was named as the capital of the Dakota Territory.

Todd was elected to serve as a delegate to the thirty-seventh and thirty-eighth Congress, representing the Dakota Territory. He served from 1861 to 1865, when he lost his bid for reelection and returned to Yankton. Locally he served as speaker of the territorial House of Representatives in 1866 and 1867. Todd passed away in 1872 in Yankton, but his legacy as the catalyst for the Dakota Territory lives on today.

As an organized territory, the Dakota Territory fell under the jurisdiction of the US government. Because there was now a governing force, much of the lawlessness and vigilante lifestyle tapered off. The Dakota

Territory was governed by the Constitution, which granted the citizens within the territory the same rights as those enjoyed by citizens in the country's eastern states. Towns like Deadwood saw more law enforcement and an increase in fair trials, and its citizens were allowed better representation in their own government.

During this time the territory saw some growth, although it was not as expansive as what other territories experienced. This was largely because early settlers encountered the hostile Sioux, who were considered a threat to anyone who ventured into the territory. The US government's violation of several treaties fueled the Sioux's discontent about white settlers' encroachment on land that had originally been granted to them.

In time the Sioux were demoralized and defeated, making the area more attractive to white settlers. The arrival of the Northern Pacific and Chicago & Northwestern railroads increased growth substantially. Many of the settlers came in large groups from other western territories, leaving their entire eastern US villages to start new lives on the frontier. Many northern and western Europeans also settled in Dakota Territory, including large numbers of Norwegians, Swedes, and Germans.

The geography of the Dakota Territory was well suited for farming because of the fertile soil and abundant streams. As the population grew, wheat farming, mining, and cattle ranching became the main sources of income for settlers, and when the Black Hills gold rush hit the area, many merchants and hoteliers ventured into the territory as well.

The Dakota Territory remained quite large until 1868, when Montana and Wyoming territories were removed. At that point Dakota Territory was reduced to the present-day boundaries of North and South Dakota.

THE DEATH OF A LEGEND
Sitting Bull's Last Days

1890

It began when the great Hunkpapa and Lakota leader Sitting Bull awoke in a cold sweat one night after experiencing his own death in a dream. A proud and visionary leader, Sitting Bull feared for his life after awaking; in the nightmare, his life was ended in an altercation with his own people. His terror proved to be prophetic.

Sitting Bull had been touring with Buffalo Bill's Wild West Show for four months before choosing to return to the Standing Rock Reservation. Once at Standing Rock, Sitting Bull reunited with most of his original band of Lakota and Hunkpapa. During this time Sitting Bull and other Lakota were beginning to practice the Ghost Dance religion, which had been founded on peaceful principles, including the cohabitation of Anglos and Native Americans. However, many homesteaders and members of the US government feared the Lakota were interpreting the Ghost Dance religion to mean a "renewed earth." This meant "washing away all the evil"—and according to the Lakota, the real evil was the intrusion of Anglos on the lands that had once belonged to the Lakota and Hunkpapa peoples.

The US government didn't help matters when it broke a Lakota treaty by changing the boundaries of the Great Sioux Reservation. Breaking this treaty gave the government the power to create five smaller reservations. This separated many families and broke tribal unions. The US policy at the time was to officially disband tribal relationships, peacefully or not, to make room for encroaching homesteaders. Sitting Bull and the Lakotas' Ghost Dance religion created unease, justified or not, for the US government.

The Ghost Dance was a dancing ritual performed in a circular fashion that would last until many of the dancers collapsed from exhaustion. Believers felt their physical sacrifice would ensure the return of the dead. Many of the religion's followers had lost husbands, warriors, and friends in battles with the US government. The hope of a renewed relationship with their ancestors sustained their belief in the Ghost Dance.

The religion came from Wovoka, a Paiute Indian "messiah." Sitting Bull and his brother, Short Bull, had visited the mystic. Wovoka's intentions when meeting with Sitting Bull and Short Bull were peaceful, just as the message of his Ghost Dance was all about peace between Indians and Anglos. But as more and more Sioux began to practice the Ghost Dance, homesteaders, Indian agents, and the US government grew more nervous. Some agents were so afraid of the new dances that they wired Washington, DC, for more military backup.

One of the Lakota chiefs, Kicking Bear, was a prominent leader in the Ghost Dance movement. Kicking Bear and Sitting Bull were at Standing Rock together. At first, Sitting Bull felt comfortable with the increasing frequency of Ghost Dance rituals, even though he doubted that the dance would actually return the dead to the living.

While he had no personal objections to the dances and the religion, the growing anxiety of the homesteaders and soldiers made him nervous as well. Sitting Bull was afraid the US government would be called in to kill more of his band.

Kicking Bear showed less fear. In fact, he encouraged more dancers to wear special shirts with painted "magic" symbols on them; some believed these symbols would repel bullets if the soldiers were to attack.

As fears increased on both sides, so did the amount of Ghost Dances performed and the number of soldiers brought into Standing Rock. Tensions reached a level that approached hysteria as Lakota wore their Ghost Dance regalia nonstop, and soldiers were at the ready around the clock. Eventually Kicking Bear was forced to leave Standing Rock. This had no effect on the number of dancers, or on the amount of dances they performed. The leading agents of the reservation asked for more troops.

Agent Valentine McGillycuddy felt unafraid and seemed to understand the religious ceremonies. A surgeon by trade, McGillycuddy was respected for his insight into the delicate relationship between the Sioux and the US government. After Kicking Bear was removed, McGillycuddy wired his superior officers with his observations:

> *The coming of the troops has frightened the Indians. If the Seventh-Day Adventists prepare the ascension robes for the Second Coming of the Savior, the United States Army is not put in motion to prevent them. Why should not the Indians have the same privilege? If the troops remain, trouble is sure to come.*

As with Sitting Bull's nightmare, McGillycuddy's sentiments would prove to be prophetic.

The majority of the agents felt Sitting Bull was at the root of the dances and responsible for their continued growth. They had blamed Sitting Bull in their formal request for additional troops, and despite the fact that this was a false accusation, their request was granted, and thousands of troops were deployed to Standing Rock.

On December 12 an order was given to arrest Sitting Bull. Two days later an officer from nearby Grand River arrived at agency headquarters with a letter announcing that Sitting Bull was making plans to leave the reservation. The letter stated:

> *That Sitting Bull was making preparations to leave the reservation; that he had fitted his horses for a long and hard ride, and that if he got the start of them, he being well mounted, the police would be unable to overtake him, and he, therefore, wanted permission to make the arrest at once.*

This letter was received and read by Standing Rock agent James McLaughlin. Upon reading this account, McLaughlin felt immediate action was necessary. Two days later, he dispatched a force of thirty-nine Indian policemen and four volunteers, one of which was Sitting Bull's brother-in-law, Gray Eagle.

The posse entered Sitting Bull's camp at daybreak, in a freezing rain. They surrounded Sitting Bull's home, knocked, and entered, telling Sitting Bull that he was under arrest and would be traveling to the agency headquarters. After Sitting Bull had dressed for the journey from his home to agency headquarters, his son Crow Foot began to yell at him. Crow Foot was furious at his father for taking the arrest so peacefully, and demanded that his father stay.

By now, Sitting Bull was fully dressed and ready to go; he had no choice but to walk past his screaming and defiant son. Soon, many members of Sitting Bull's family and tribe were on the scene and curious. In seeing his family and his tribal members in disgust, Sitting Bull grew impatient and refused to mount the horse. The posse tired of Sitting Bull's resistance and used force. As Sitting Bull demanded help from onlookers, the police tried to calm the crowd, and eventually forced them back.

Two different accounts attempt to explain what happened next, but neither provides conclusive evidence. It does seem clear that a large, close-quarters fight resulted. One account says a Sioux, Catch the Bear, shouldered his rifle as the police wrestled with Sitting Bull. Catch the Bear supposedly shot a Lieutenant Bull Head, who then fired his revolver at close range into the chest of Sitting Bull. Upon seeing that, another police officer felt Sitting Bull was not dead enough, so he shot the Sioux chief in the head.

A second account said that Sitting Bull called for the growing crowd of Sioux to attack the police. According to this account, Catch the Bear and Strike the Kettle exploded from the crowd and fired at Lieutenant Bull Head, who, at the time, was standing next to Sitting Bull. When Catch the Bear fired at Bull Head, Bull Head then shot Sitting Bull in the ribs.

Both accounts describe an ensuing bloodbath of hand-to-hand combat that lasted for nearly an hour. E. G. Fechet, captain of the 8th Cavalry, reported that the arrest of Sitting Bull was commendable:

> *I cannot too strongly commend the splendid courage and ability which characterized the conduct of the Indian police commanded by Bull Head and Shave Head throughout the encounter. The attempt to arrest Sitting Bull was so managed as to place the responsibility for the fight that ensued upon Sitting Bull's band, which began the firing. Red Tomahawk assumed command of the police after both Bull Head and Shave Head had been wounded, and it was he who, under circumstances requiring personal courage to the highest degree, assisted Hawk Man to escape with a message to the troops. After the fight, no demoralization seemed to exist among them, and they were ready and willing to cooperate with the troops to any extent desired.*

As the sun grew higher in the December sky and turned the freezing rain into a cold drizzle, eighteen men lay dead. Sitting Bull and his son were among them.

McLaughlin described the successful arrest in his report to the United States Indian Service: "Everything is now quiet at this Agency," he penned, "and good feeling prevails among the Indians, Newspaper reports to the contrary notwithstanding."

TEXAS

A CARGO OF CAMELS

1856

Residents of Indianola, Texas, had looked forward for almost two weeks to this day, May 14, 1856. They had heard rumors that a ship was floating just a few miles out in the Gulf of Mexico, waiting for the sea to calm so that she could dock at one of the long wharves that jutted into Matagorda Bay. Indianola was among the best seaports in the Lone Star State, and the town's citizens were used to seeing ships from all countries come and go. But today would be unique. Today the incoming ship carried a cargo few Texans had ever seen: camels!

All morning, curious spectators gathered at the docks and strained to spot the naval vessel on the far horizon. The news was that the *Supply*—the ship that had carried the animals across the Atlantic Ocean from the Middle East—was going to bring the camels into port.

Then the harbormaster received word that, because of bad weather in the gulf, the *Supply* had rendezvoused with another ship, the *Fashion*, off the coast of Louisiana and had transferred the camels to it. Finally, just before noon, the *Fashion* put into port at Indianola.

Almost the entire population of the town watched in amazement as the sailors aboard the *Fashion* dropped a gangplank and started leading the camels down the incline to the dock. According to Major Henry C. Wayne, the officer in charge of the strange cargo, the animals, once their feet hit dry ground, "became excited to an almost uncontrolled degree, rearing, kicking, crying out, breaking halters, tearing up pickets and by other fantastic tricks demonstrating their enjoyment of the 'Liberty of the soil.'"

The long trip over the Mediterranean, through the Strait of Gibraltar, and across the Atlantic Ocean had been relatively uneventful considering the fragile cargo the *Supply* had on board. Navy Lieutenant David D. Porter, who later gained fame in the Civil War as a Union admiral, had been responsible for acquiring the camels in the Middle East, and one of the first chores he performed upon returning home was to notify US Secretary of War Jefferson Davis of his success. He wrote:

> *We have lost on the voyage but one of those we purchased . . . and she died from no want of care, but because she was not able to produce her young one. . . . We still have more than we started with, some young ones having been born on the passage, and are in fine condition. All the other camels I am happy to say have not received a scratch. . . . [T]hey are looking a little shabby just now, most of them shedding their hair . . . but they are fat and in good health.*

A year earlier, the US Congress, at Davis's urging, had authorized "the importation of camels and dromedaries to be used for military purposes" and had earmarked thirty thousand dollars for the experiment. Davis, a veteran of the war with Mexico, had seen considerable service in the desert Southwest. Keenly aware of the role that camels had played over the centuries in the warfare of other nations, he believed that the strange beasts could be put to good use in the United States as well.

After considerable planning, Major Wayne and Lieutenant Porter departed for North Africa, where they were met by a third American, Gwinn Harris Heap, whose father had been US consul to Tunis for a number of years. After visiting several cities along the Mediterranean coast, the threesome acquired thirty-three camels before departing for home in February 1856.

Indianola was ready for the camels. Ten acres of land had been set aside for them, and a two-hundred-foot-long shed had been built to house them. Major Wayne decided first to acclimate the animals to the intense humidity of the Gulf Coast by letting them rest awhile in a large corral. Three weeks later, he assembled the animals for a 140-mile journey to San Antonio, the first leg of a trip that would eventually take them to El Paso, Albuquerque, and across the arid Southwest all the way to Fort Tejon, California.

To the amazement of all concerned, the camels performed extremely well. Capable of carrying loads of up to twelve hundred pounds—more than a horse or mule could carry—the beasts of burden lumbered along at a slow but steady pace across the trackless desert. In an effort to establish a breeding program for the camels, Wayne, who had gone on to a desk job in Washington, DC, wrote to Quartermaster General Thomas J. Jesup:

> *I have never entertained the idea, that the benefits to be derived from the introduction of the animal among us could be so extensively realized in our day. I regard it more in the light of a legacy to posterity of precisely the same character as the introduction of the horse and other domestic animals by the early settlers of America have been to us.*

But the great camel experiment eventually failed. With the advent of the Civil War, the personnel at Union garrisons in the Southwest scattered before the advancing Confederates. Matters more important than the formulation and maintenance of a camel corps soon occupied the minds of Union commanders. Some of the imported camels were set free and some were kept in captivity. The last known survivor died in a Los Angeles zoo in 1934, but even today people occasionally tell tales of seeing lone camels in remote corners of the Southwest.

BILLY DIXON'S REMARKABLE SHOT

1874

If there was one facet of Billy Dixon's life of which he was most proud, it was his career as a buffalo hunter, or more specifically a hide hunter. Although he was only twenty-three years old, he had already won the admiration and respect of hunters many years his senior. He was known all over Texas, Kansas, and Indian Territory for his marksmanship and his ability to bring down staggering numbers of buffalo in the course of a single day.

But on June 29, 1874, Dixon wasn't thinking about buffalo. The young hunter was concerned about his safety and that of his twenty-five or so companions. For the past three days, they had been holed up at a remote hunters' camp in the Texas Panhandle called Adobe Walls, fighting off a brutal attack by Comanche, Kiowa, and Cheyenne warriors under the leadership of Isa-tai and Quanah Parker. Three men had already died in the fierce fighting, which pitted the handful of hunters against nearly seven hundred Indians. The warriors had also shot and killed most of the hunters' horses and cattle. Had it not been for the thick walls of sod, more casualties would likely have occurred inside Adobe Walls.

For two days after the initial attack, it had been fairly quiet in the hunters' compound. One man slipped away to Dodge City for help, while a burial detail interred the three dead men in a single grave. The hunters also disposed of the rotting carcasses of the cattle and horses as best they could. The Indians still surrounded Adobe Walls at a distance, showing themselves from time to time to remind the men inside that escape was impossible.

While several of the hunters surveyed the plain around the camp, they noticed some Indians silhouetted against a slight rise about a mile away. One of the hunters was Dixon, who had lost his prize Sharps rifle several days earlier while crossing the swollen Canadian River. Now, he reached over and picked up James Hanrahan's .50-caliber Sharps and fiddled for a moment with the rear sights. He aimed the rifle at a lone Indian outlined against the skyline. The big Sharps belched flames and smoke. Neither Dixon, his friends, nor the Indian's companions could believe their eyes. Dixon later described the incident:

> *I took careful aim and pulled the trigger. We saw an Indian fall from his horse. The others dashed out of sight and behind a clump of timber. A few moments later two Indians ran quickly on foot to where the dead Indian lay, seized his body and scurried for cover. They had risked their lives, as we had frequently observed, to rescue a companion who might be not only wounded, but dead. I was admittedly a good marksman, yet this was what might be called a scratch shot.*

Dixon's fluke shot was too much for the Indians. They left Adobe Walls to the buffalo hunters. Once they were out of sight, a curious hunter paced off the distance of Dixon's remarkable shot and found that it was 1,538 yards—nearly seven-eighths of a mile!

Out of the dramatic battle at Adobe Walls, two legends were born. One concerned the marksmanship of Billy Dixon. Although he repeatedly acknowledged that he had been lucky, his marksmanship became a subject for storytellers forever after.

Dixon went on to become a distinguished scout for the Sixth US Cavalry under the command of Colonel Nelson Miles. He was awarded a Medal of Honor in 1874 for his "skill, courage and determined fortitude, displayed in an engagement with 5 others, on the 12th of September, 1874, against hostile Indians in overwhelming numbers." The US Army later rescinded the award after learning that Dixon had been a civilian at the time.

The other legend spawned by Adobe Walls was the accuracy and killing power of the Sharps rifle. The Sharps had already been used by both North and South during the Civil War, but it was the hide hunters who made it so popular. It was the weapon of choice for hundreds of buffalo hunters who scoured the Great Plains in search of ever-dwindling herds during the 1870s and 1880s. To these men, the beauty of the Sharps was its ability to fire a heavy bullet several hundred yards with complete accuracy. Since the hunters usually shot their prey from a distance of at least three hundred yards, to keep from spooking other members of the herd, the long-range Sharps was ideal. Its reputation continued to grow as tales of Dixon's mile-long shot spread.

By the 1880s, buffalo had all but disappeared from the southern Great Plains. One reason for the mass extinction was hide hunters such as Dixon wielding sure-fire weapons such as the Sharps rifle. But another factor entered into the equation. The US government condoned the slaughter of the once-numerous bison as a means of controlling and "civilizing" the various Plains Indian tribes who depended upon the animal for their livelihood.

In 1875, when Texas legislators were considering a bill to protect the last of the state's buffalo herds, General Philip Sheridan appeared before the lawmakers and urged them to kill the proposal. In Sheridan's opinion, the men who destroyed the buffalo were heroes. They should be given "a hearty, unanimous vote of thanks," he said, as well as a bronze medal "with a dead buffalo on one side and a discouraged Indian on the other." Sheridan continued:

> *These men have done in the last two years, and will do in the next year, more to settle the vexed Indian question than the entire regular army has done in the last twenty years. They are destroying the Indians' commissary; and it is a well-known fact that an army losing its base of supplies is placed at a great disadvantage. Send them the powder and lead, if you will; but for the sake of a lasting peace, let them kill, skin and sell until the buffaloes are exterminated. Then your prairies can be covered with speckled cattle and the festive cowboy, who follows the hunter as a second forerunner of an advanced civilization.*

SAN ANTONIO

ROUGH RIDING

1898

The men stood around the corral as the bucking iron-gray wild horse was brought into the ring. Here was the second in command of their regiment, a New Yorker, stepping up to break the horse. The men were skeptical and nudged each other at the prospect of what this city fellow was getting himself into. The horse seemed to be the leader of this wild herd of fifteen hundred; only one in a hundred of these wild horses had ever had a rope on him. He had a fierce look in his eye—bespeaking that he would rather kill someone than be ridden. His fight was a force to be reckoned with. Still, Theodore Roosevelt called out that he wanted the iron gray. The men had all wondered who would have to break him for their leader, but to their surprise he got a rope, made an underhanded throw—the most difficult—and got the horse on the first try. Some thought it was a first timer's luck, but then Roosevelt quickly proved himself as a fine horseman. He began to hip the horse down, blindfolded him with his own bandanna, and saddled him. Then he mounted the horse, and the men said with awe that they witnessed such bucking and riding as they had never seen before. The murmur of their astonishment led to the word that he had once been a Montana rancher as well as a

New York cop. In their chagrin, the men went up and apologized for not treating Roosevelt the way that they should have, but he shrugged it off like he didn't know what they were talking about. They soon found that this leadership in the ring was made of character that would inspire great trust and admiration. He had what it took to tame a wild horse and lead a motley crew. Any of them would have laid down their life for him.

The men were part of the First US Volunteer Cavalry Regiment, a mix of the New York elite (some of Roosevelt's Harvard classmates), American Indians, Texas cowboys, rangers, miners, and drifters—a mix of young American manhood—enlisted to fight in the Spanish American War. The training ground was in San Antonio. Roosevelt had been assistant secretary of the navy but resigned to become second in command with the rank of lieutenant colonel under his friend Colonel Leonard Wood. The cavalry became known as the Rough Riders after a Washington correspondent described them as a "rough riding outfit." As they arrived in San Antonio, some of the locals called them "Teddy's terrors."

When Colonel Wood first arrived in 1898, he set up recruitment headquarters in the patio of the Menger Hotel, and many recruits camped nearby on the old Alamo mission grounds. Wood soon moved the whole operation to the International Fairgrounds. Roosevelt joined him eleven days later by train, and after breakfast at the Menger, Wood found him and off they went to the training grounds. Roosevelt found twelve of his Harvard classmates hard at work digging trenches and serving in the kitchen, joining right in with the work of the camp. When the twelve had arrived the day before, they too had eaten at the Menger. The hotel register was likened to an invitation list to a New York society ball.

The troops were outfitted in slouch hats, blue flannel shirts, brown trousers, leggings, and boots. To top off their cowboy look, bandannas were knotted around their necks. Roosevelt wrote much later that the men were what gave the group its "peculiar character and reputation. These Southwesterners, naturally, many from Texas slipped in, gave us a ready-made group of fighters who could ride and shoot and take orders."

Not all registered under their real names, as some seemed to have been associated with "fierce crimes." As a regiment, they were a tough fighting force to be reckoned with. The Rough Riders were only in San Antonio for a month, but they made quite an impression in the Menger Bar and at less respected sections of town. Roosevelt and his friend, New York socialite Cornelius Vanderbilt, were said to have galloped their horses right up to the hotel entrance to join the revelry.

They joined the war efforts, as short as they were, and became notorious for their charge up San Juan Hill. Though trained as cavalry, they found upon arrival in Florida that only the officers could take their horses; all the greater was their bravery as they fought as foot soldiers. They lost many valiant young men and suffered many casualties, but through it all Roosevelt stayed with his men.

Roosevelt went on to a life of politics, first as vice-president and then the twenty-sixth president after the assassination of President William McKinley. He was a fighter but also a foreign policy strategist who received a Nobel Peace Prize. He returned to the Menger Hotel in 1905 for a Rough Riders reunion. In 1998 another commemoration of the Rough Riders took place to celebrate the one-hundredth anniversary of the founding of this cavalry of wild men. Now the Menger Bar has been renamed in the former president's honor as the Roosevelt Bar. It commemorates the coming together of volunteer young men from the elite and ordinary classes as one unit famous for its peculiar character as a cavalry regiment, its reputation for being as wild on the field as in the watering holes of San Antonio's frontier town, and for the leader who earned their respect in the breaking of a fierce iron-gray horse.

UTAH

DRIVING THE GOLDEN SPIKE

1869

Sitting in the midst of Utah's northwestern desert, desolate Promontory Summit gives little indication that it is one of the most significant sites in the history of the United States. Little about the place has changed since this 1869 account: "The town consists of a few tents, the ticket houses of both companies, their telegraph offices, hordes of grasshoppers and swarms of sand fleas."

Yet, at 12:47 p.m. on May 10, 1869, history was made at Promontory Summit when a golden spike was driven through a tie to complete the first transcontinental railroad in the United States.

The country would never be the same, and those at Promontory Summit that morning knew it. Travelers could now ride from New York to California in six days and twenty-two minutes. Before the two rail lines connected, travel from Independence, Missouri, to Sacramento, California, had taken six months by wagon train. Businessmen could now ship grain or cattle to markets on either coast quickly and easily. Settlers would soon fill in the vast spaces in the West and would stimulate business with their needs for goods and services.

The railroad magnates, Central Pacific's Leland Stanford and Union Pacific's Thomas Durant, had plenty to celebrate. They had overcome many obstacles, Congress's bickering not the least among them. Despite the turmoil of the Civil War, the railroaders had persuaded their legislators to authorize the building of the transcontinental line.

The project began in 1863. Stanford's Central Pacific Railroad had started in California, laying track eastward from Sacramento. The Union Pacific Railroad headed west from Omaha. Congress gave each railroad ten alternate sections of land and subsidized loans of between sixteen thousand and forty-eight thousand dollars for each mile of track.

The men who actually built the railroad were a mixed population; their demographics reveal much about American society in the 1860s. Irish, German, and Italian immigrants joined ex-Civil War veterans from both sides of the conflict along with freed slaves to work for the Union Pacific. The mixture of races, nationalities, and loyalties among soldiers made this an interesting group that did not get along easily.

The Central Pacific imported ten thousand Chinese laborers to build its tracks. The terrain—which included the Sierra Nevada Mountains and the scorching Great Basin Desert—was difficult at best. To complicate matters further, all the Central Pacific's materials, including rails, spikes, and locomotives, had to be shipped fifteen thousand miles around Cape Horn.

Many people compromised to bring about the celebration at Promontory Summit that morning. As the two railroads neared completion, they passed each other without connecting tracks. Bickering and profiteering led to building more than two hundred miles of railroad on nearly parallel grades. Congress finally intervened, ordering the rails to be joined at Promontory Summit on May 10, 1869.

Some early newspaper stories said the rails would be joined at Promontory Point, a spot about thirty-five miles away from Promontory Summit. To this day, many Utahns and even some American history textbooks perpetuate the myth of Promontory Point.

The plans for the celebration underwent change and compromise too. Neither of the locomotives that brought Durant and Stanford to the historic spot—the Central Pacific's *Jupiter* and the Union Pacific's *119*—were scheduled to star in the big occasion.

Leland Stanford had planned to arrive in a train pulled by a special locomotive called the *Antelope*. As Stanford's locomotive approached its destination, railroad workers failed to notice the small green flag that signaled the arrival of another train, and they had rolled a log down the cut near the tracks. The *Antelope* hit the log and was too damaged to use. Railroad officials elected to couple the Central Pacific dignitaries' cars to a regular engine. The substitute engine, *Jupiter*, took the *Antelope*'s place in the famous photo of the "Wedding of the Rails" snapped by Andrew J. Russell.

The Union Pacific also pressed a substitute locomotive into service in the last hours of the adventure. History doesn't record the name of the engine that should have brought Durant to Promontory Summit, but the combination of a rickety wooden bridge and the swollen Weber River knocked the chosen locomotive out of the running. That engine was far too heavy to safely cross the bridge at Devils Gate, east of Ogden, so the cars carrying Durant and his party were detached from the engine and pushed across the bridge. Once the cars were safely on the other side, the *119* picked them up and transported them to the historic meeting site. (The bridge was strengthened later for regular railroad traffic.)

The celebration itself was lengthy and awkward. The dignitaries gave interminable speeches, congratulating themselves on achieving the historic linkage. Durant, apparently still recovering from the party the night before, left the group for a short time. Grenville Dodge, the Union Pacific's chief engineer, stepped in to give Durant's speech. Durant later returned to finish the ceremony.

The workers watched as two golden spikes were presented to Stanford, who dropped them into the first and fourth predrilled holes in a laurelwood tie. Durant put a silver spike donated by the State of Nevada and a gold-silver-iron-alloy spike donated by the State of Arizona in the other two holes. The precious metal spikes and laurelwood tie were then removed and replaced with a regular tie and four iron spikes.

At the proper moment, the dignitaries were supposed to drive in the final iron spike. This spike was wired to the telegraph. Three ticks on the telegraph would signal to the whole country that the railroad was finished. But the "big men" of the railroad, who were used to wielding fountain pens instead of mauls, kept missing the mark. The workers rolled with laughter.

James Strobridge, supervisor of the Chinese construction crews, finally drove in the last spike. The telegraph operator sent a simple four-letter message—D-O-N-E. At long last, the transcontinental railroad had been completed. Together, railroad crews from the Union Pacific and Central Pacific Railroads crossed 1,776 miles of rugged and often hostile terrain. The United States was united by rail for the first time.

These days, exact replicas of the *Jupiter* and the *119* puff out of their engine house at the Golden Spike National Historic Site (managed by the National Park Service) during the summer months; at other times of the year, visitors view the locomotives inside a large garage. A reenactment ceremony occurs annually on May 10. A variety of films, exhibits, hikes, and interpretive drives celebrate the joining of the rails.

MARTHA HUGHES
CANNON WINS A RACE

1896

Martha Hughes Cannon had a great deal riding on the 1896 election: years of hard work, her future, and perhaps her marriage. She and her husband were both running for the Utah state legislature. Fortunately, they weren't running head to head. Voters would elect five state senators out of a field of ten. So it was possible that both Martha and her husband, Angus Cannon, would win.

People thought it was nice that this husband and wife had politics in common. Angus was a Republican and Martha was a Democrat, but Martha and Angus respected each other and publicly supported each other's candidacy. Any way the election went, the public would be watching to see what happened between them. A woman running for office was sensational enough; how much more exciting to watch her run against her husband!

It was an interesting year in Utah politics. Utah had become a state the previous January. This was the first chance Utahns would have to vote for a president of the United States. The election for state senate was just as important. The state senators, not the public, would choose those who would represent Utah in the United States Senate.

If a woman running for office was unusual in the 1890s, so was the idea of women voting in elections. Nationally, women did not earn the right to vote until 1920. But Utah women had been voting since 1870—except for a nine-year period when the United States government had taken the right away. Contrary to national practice, Utah included the women's right to vote in its state constitution. Utah women had been active in politics for a long time. Martha was not the only woman candidate in 1896; seven women were running for the Utah state legislature. The Democrat-Populist party and the Republican Party could each nominate five candidates for state senate. Martha was nominated by the Democratic-Populist convention to represent the twenty-second precinct of Salt Lake County. In his nominating speech for Martha, L. R. Letcher praised her as both a graduate of two medical colleges and a "womanly woman." He assured the voters that she would vote the party line and dared any man to vote against her. Martha garnered more votes than any other nominee at the convention. The Democratic Party felt it was important to show their support for women's suffrage.

Meanwhile, the Republican convention nominated Angus Cannon to run for state senate. For another of their five nominees, the Republicans also chose a woman, Martha's good friend and fellow suffragist Emmeline B. Wells. Martha Cannon was in a tough spot, running against both her friend and her husband.

Martha was worried—not about her marriage, but about the election. She feared that voters would not want a husband and wife to work together and would vote for her husband instead of her. She knew also that many Gentiles (non-Mormons) would refuse to vote for her because she was a Mormon polygamist's wife.

Her husband could feel confident of his election because he was the Mormon state president in Salt Lake County, a prestigious and visible position. Cannon had six wives; Martha was his fourth. He had married Martha in 1884 in a secret ceremony because the federal government had begun to persecute polygamists. A few months after the marriage, federal agents caught up with Angus Cannon, and he had spent time in prison. Now, each of Angus's wives had her own household. Angus chose to live with none of them so the marshals could not arrest him again.

Martha and Angus had two children together. After the birth of her first child, Martha left the country to keep attention away from Angus. When the persecution of polygamists died down, Martha returned to Utah and immersed herself in the women's suffrage movement. She, Emmeline B. Wells, and others had worked to include women's right to vote in Utah's state constitution.

The 1896 campaign was long and hard. Martha traveled to Granger, Brigham City, South Taylorsville, Draper, the Third Municipal Ward, and even the Old Soldier's meeting to speak. Each speech exhorted citizens to vote Democratic. She asked for votes for her ideas, not her gender. Martha supported the Democratic candidate for president of the United States, William Jennings Bryan, over Republican William McKinley.

The hot national issue was the campaign for free coinage and silver. Both presidential candidate Bryan and the Utah Democratic Party were strongly opposed to the gold standard in the United States. The Republicans supported the standard. Martha promised, if she were elected, to vote for a senator who would oppose the gold standard in Congress.

The Utah Republican Party had split over the silver coinage debate. It cost them the election. Bryan carried Utah. The citizens didn't elect a single Republican to the state senate. Angus Cannon lost to former territorial representative John T. Caine. Martha came in with the least number of votes in her party, but she won the race. She had received 2,671 more votes than Angus. Angus bore his disappointment well, saying he had always supported his wife.

Martha Hughes Cannon became the first woman state senator in the history of the United States. When a journalist asked how this made her feel, Martha replied that she had not thought much about her place in history, but she would have to try to live up to her privileges.

With Martha Cannon's notoriety, a spotlight was cast on her polygamous marriage. Many suffragists felt that polygamy was a plot by men to keep women enslaved. Martha countered that polygamy was an essential part of her religion, and she wished to live her faith fully. She also suggested that women who share their husband have more independence.

Health was a great interest of Senator Cannon's. She had spent most of her life training as a doctor and had received degrees in medicine and elocution. She met Angus while working as a resident physician at Deseret Hospital; he was on the board of directors. Martha had seen many women and children die because of the unhealthy condition of their lives. She was determined to do something about it.

As a freshman politician, Martha Cannon sponsored and passed three bills the first month. Senate Bill 31 improved the condition of women salesclerks; it mandated that stools or chairs be provided so the women would not have to stand all day. Senate Bill 22 allocated money for the education of sight- and hearing-impaired children. Senate Bill 27 created a Utah State Board of Health. The seven-member board would help establish local boards statewide that would improve sanitation, establish a clean water supply, and control disease. The legislation Cannon introduced probably saved many lives.

During her second year as senator, Martha was pregnant with her third child. She was also chairing the Public Health Committee. That year, she sponsored Senate Bill 40, which set up greater protections against infectious diseases, and Senate Bill 1, which authorized construction of a hospital for the Utah State School for the Deaf and Dumb. She tried but failed to pass a bill to mandate teaching the harmful effects of drugs and alcohol to schoolchildren.

When her two-session term was up, Cannon did not run again. Governor Heber Wells had appointed her to serve on the State Board of

Health. She worked for the welfare of the state from that position and started a medical practice of her own.

During its centennial celebration in 1996, the state honored Martha Cannon's accomplishments with a statue in the Utah State Capitol. Utah did not elect another woman state senator until twenty-three years later. Today, Utah women remain a visible minority on Capitol Hill.

WASHINGTON

INDIAN WARS

1858

Lieutenant Colonel William Jenner Steptoe, a forty-two-year-old graduate of West Point, marched from the stockade walls of Fort Walla Walla, Washington Territory, on May 6, 1858, with 164 men of the First Dragoons and the Ninth Infantry. Included in the column were a surgeon, a commissary officer, several civilian packers, a few friendly Nez Perce Indians, and two twelve-pound mountain howitzers. Their destination was the mining region around Colville, a small settlement almost two hundred miles north of the fort in the land between the Pend Oreille and Columbia Rivers.

Steptoe, an experienced officer from Virginia and a veteran of the Seminole and Mexican Wars, had been assigned to Washington Territory since 1854, shortly after being offered—and refusing—the governorship of Utah Territory. Almost from Steptoe's arrival, Washington Territory had been a hotbed of activity for several dissatisfied Indian groups, among them the Yakima, Spokane, Palous, and Coeur d'Alene tribes. Most of the Indians' unhappiness stemmed from the continuing encroachment upon tribal lands by white settlers and miners.

Territorial Governor Isaac I. Stevens, a former army officer and railroad surveyor, had set the stage for much of the unrest in the region. In May 1855 Stevens had negotiated treaties with about five thousand Indians of several tribes in the Walla Walla Valley. During a long and grueling meeting, the Indians had finally signed away most of their ancestral lands for a pittance. After promising the tribesmen that they could retain their homeland for several more years—until the treaty was ratified—less than two weeks later Stevens announced the opening of the Indian lands to white settlement.

In September 1856 the construction of Fort Walla Walla signified the army's intention to become a permanent presence in the region. By 1858 the influx of thousands of American miners and farmers into the eastern parts of Washington Territory had intensified the animosity the Indians felt toward whites. When Steptoe received a request from miners in the Colville region for protection against a suspected Indian uprising in the area, he responded by marching a column of soldiers north to negotiate with the Indians. This provided just the right heat for the pot to boil over.

On his way to Colville, Steptoe and his command were met by a contingent of several hundred Palous, Spokane, and Coeur d'Alene warriors who demanded that the soldiers leave natives' land and return to Fort Walla Walla. On May 17 Steptoe agreed to the Indians' request and turned his column south toward his command post. The Indians, in the meantime, had worked themselves into a frenzy, and even though Steptoe's command was working its way slowly southward, the Indians attacked the rear and sides of the column. Retreating to a knoll, Steptoe and his men fought off repeated assaults until dusk.

When Steptoe's command had left Fort Walla Walla earlier in the month, the colonel had cut the ammunition ration to each soldier to forty rounds, due to the extreme weight of the rest of the equipment and supplies that had to be carried on the backs of the pack animals. Now, after fighting all day, the men were down to three rounds each. Steptoe and his officers decided to leave the howitzers, camp supplies, and extra animals behind and to descend the butte under cover of darkness and rapidly retreat to safety.

Jack Dodd, the battle's historian, summarized the outcome of the battle in *Great Western Indian Fights.*

> *Two weeks had elapsed since the expedition had left. . . . In that time Steptoe's men had fought gallantly against a foe that outnumbered them eight to one, and had miraculously escaped from an almost certain massacre. The final losses were two officers, ten men, and three friendly Indians killed, plus ten men wounded, and 29 horses killed or lost from wounds in the "Battle of Tohoto-nim-me." The exact hostile losses are not known, but acknowledged losses were nine killed and 40 or 50 wounded.*

News of Steptoe's less than successful encounter with the Indians was met with disbelief among the authorities in the army's Department of the Pacific. Orders were immediately sent out to organize a new company, this time to be led by fifty-five-year-old Colonel George Wright, a longtime army regular and veteran of the Seminole and Mexican Wars, as well as of administrative duties as commander of the District of Columbia. Heading up several companies of the Ninth Infantry, the First Dragoons, and the Third Artillery, Wright left Fort Walla Walla on August 15, 1858, following several units of his command that had left previously to build a fort at the crossing of the Snake River. In all, close to seven hundred men and eight hundred animals accompanied Wright on his mission to exact retribution from the Indians who had sent Steptoe and his forces scurrying back to Fort Walla Walla.

Colonel Wright ordered his command to pitch camp at Four Lakes on the night of August 31, following a day that had been marked by increased Indian activity in the area. They were just a few miles southwest of today's bustling city of Spokane. By dawn of the next day, the Indians had occupied a nearby hill, and after a display of strength by the army, the Indians retreated down the north slope, taunting the soldiers all the way. Wright deployed various elements of his command, dislodging the Indians from their new post at the foot of the hill and sending the enemy into retreat. No US Army soldiers were lost in this conflict known as the Battle of Four Lakes. About twenty Indians were killed and many more wounded.

Colonel Wright then marched northward and engaged the Indians again on September 5, in the Battle of Spokane Plains. As in the affair at Four Lakes, the army's sword-wielding dragoons, menacing artillery, and new, more accurate rifles used by the soldiers were too much for the Indian warriors, who were armed only with spears, bows and arrows, and inaccurate trade rifles.

After the wars of 1858 were over and the Indians realized that they were no match for the superior weaponry of the US Army, peace, more or less, returned to Washington Territory. Each year that followed witnessed thousands of white emigrants flooding into the territory and taking permanent possession of what had been the Indians' ancestral lands.

SEATTLE

HERE COME THE BRIDES

1864

Asa Shinn Mercer (1839–1917) leaned against the rail of the sloop *Kidder* and sighed; the end of his long voyage drew closer with each slap of the waves against the ship's prow. A chill night's sea breeze moistened his eyes as the ship slipped east over Elliot Bay's gently rolling waves. The vague silhouette of Seattle, the small Puget Sound logging town of about a thousand people, faded into view. The flickering flames of Doc Maynard's and a small greeting party's oil lamps dotted the shoreline. Mercer had accomplished his mission: With petticoats and baggage, the New England maidens in search of new lives—and husbands—were about to step onto the shores of their new town.

Asa Mercer achieved much success during his pioneering life. As one of early Seattle's movers (literally, since he was the town's first teamster), among other accomplishments, people elected Mercer to the Territorial Legislature and, at twenty-five years old, he became president of the Territorial University of Washington. How had such a young man attained so lofty a post? By cleverly being Seattle's sole college graduate—he was also its only professor.

Although successful in Seattle, Washington, he'd eventually relocate to Cheyenne, Wyoming, where he'd gain prominence as a writer and publisher. However, the choice to leave Seattle wasn't entirely his own. In fact, if not for his brother Thomas, a judge, the Mercer name might not be so well represented on Seattle-area landmarks. But we'll get to that in a bit.

Unquestionably, there is one singular accomplishment that stands above his others in both fame and impact on Seattle's history: Asa Mercer brought lonely East Coast women to lonely West Coast men; rather than to the Territorial Legislature, if he'd have run for the position, he could have been elected king.

A booming community, 1864 Seattle suffered no shortage of loggers, miners, fishermen, craftsmen, and businessmen—with an emphasis on *men*. You've no doubt gathered a glaring gender gap among the residents of mid-1860s Seattle—tons of men, but few women of marrying age. Also, the families that had been established were producing children, who needed to be taught, and teachers at the time were normally women.

When folks consider what Asa Mercer did for Seattle, this old saw may pop into their noggin: "Everyone talks about the weather, but no one does anything about it." Everyone complained about too few eligible women in Seattle, but no one was doing anything about it. Well, Asa Mercer, a well-known doer, decided he'd *do* something about it.

Mercer knew very well where to find husbands in need of wives—they surrounded him every day—but where to find the wives? An educated man and logical thinker, Mercer relied on deduction. The Civil War had claimed hundreds of thousands of Union soldiers, many from the northeast, leaving war widows and eligible young women unattached. He decided to travel east to entice New England women to Seattle. With many husbands and eligible men killed in battle and others off fighting, unmarried women needed to earn a living. However, work was scarce as most of the textile mills had closed because cotton deliveries from the South had ceased.

From the pulpit of the Unitarian Church in Lowell, Massachusetts, Mercer cajoled the congregation with a special emphasis on the young, unmarried ladies. In the end he managed to convince eight women to sail to Seattle. One man also joined them. Mercer and his party traveled to New York, where they were joined by two additional women, a man, and another woman bound for San Francisco who would later change her mind and continue on to Seattle.

On March 14, 1864, Mercer and his entourage joined almost eight hundred other passengers aboard the S.S. *Illinois,* hoisting sails from New York for Central America. The ship passed through the Isthmus of Panama about ten days later. In Panama Mercer learned that the S.S. *America,* the ship to which they'd transfer for their remaining West Coast voyage, would be delayed by a week due to mechanical problems.

After a week's unplanned stay in Central America, the party once again set sail for California en route to the Great Pacific Northwest. Mercer learned in San Francisco that the monthly steamship aboard which they'd planned on sailing their final leg to Seattle had already left port. Not thrilled with another delay, rather than wait the better portion of a month, Mercer arranged passage on the *Torrant,* a ship known as a lumber bark.

The party first landed in Washington Territory in Teekalet (Port Gamble), on the Olympic Peninsula, to a curious greeting party. The next day they boarded the sloop *Kidder* for the final push into Seattle.

The *Kidder* pulled into the dock near midnight on April 3, 1864. The late arrival meant a small greeting party and a handheld lamp escort to Seattle's only hotel for the night. The next day the community held a reception at the university to show its appreciation for Mercer's efforts and to welcome the women who'd left their families behind for a new life in Seattle.

The first "Mercer Girls" to arrive in Seattle were:

Josephine "Josie" Pearson: schoolteacher
Georgia Pearson: schoolteacher/lighthouse keeper
Sarah Cheney: schoolteacher
Sarah J. Gallagher: university music teacher
Antoinette Baker: schoolteacher
Aurelia Coffin: schoolteacher
Lizzie Ordway: schoolteacher/school superintendent
Kate Stevens
Catherine "Kate" Stickney
Ann Murphy
Annie Adams

Mercer was emboldened but not satisfied with the small number of women who'd accompanied him to Seattle. The Puget Sound region's population had grown to about ten thousand, and his goal was eventually to bring sufficient eligible women west, where marriageable men were plentiful. Therefore, Mercer headed out on a second wife-gathering venture, but on May 28, 1866, he returned to Seattle with only forty-six eligible women. Not bad compared with the first trip, but he'd promised the men that he'd recruit at least five hundred women to embark with him on the S.S. *Continental* bound for Seattle. However, many "recruits" abandoned Mercer in force following a story in the *New York Herald* insinuating Mercer was engaging in "white slavery." Still, at least Asa Mercer couldn't have considered the endeavor a failure. A *New York Times* reporter who'd sailed west with the ship to record the voyage reported that the normally stoic Mercer had invited one of the "Mercer Belles" to his cabin, where he'd proposed marriage. The reporter asserts the unidentified woman laughed at Mercer's overture. However, Mercer may have gotten the last laugh on the reporter; he soon married passenger Annie B. Stephens.

While many considered his procurement project a pathetic failure, having delivered forty-six potential brides when he'd promised five hundred, and taking one for his own, Mercer may not have. However, his own matrimonial bliss didn't go over particularly well with the majority of lonely loggers, seamen, and miners he'd "jilted." Let's just say Asa Shinn Mercer's getting out of Seattle with his hide intact is evidence that Seattle's sheriff, who protected Mercer as he departed, must have already been married.

WYOMING

A HISTORIC VOTE

1870

She was nervous as she wrote the name down on the small square of paper. Her hand was shaking, partially as a result of those nerves and partially with the excitement of what she was about to do. Grandma Swain had come with other members of her community in the frontier town of Laramie, Wyoming, to elect a new town council. It was something she had waited all her life to do; something that no woman in her family had ever been able to do.

Elections were big events in 1870, bringing in residents of the community from all over the small town. Laramie—known as the Gem City of the Plains—was close to the border of what in six years would be the state of Colorado. The transcontinental railroad was almost completed and part of those tracks ran right through downtown Laramie. The founding fathers of Laramie hoped to take advantage of the merchandise and travelers the tracks would bring to build a first-class western town, nestled in the southeast corner of the yet-to-be-established Wyoming Territory.

It was a cool, windy day. A tent had been set up for the voting. A locked wooden box with a long, narrow slot on top rested on a wooden table. Small squares of paper were placed at the end of the table. Lead was available to write with. Two men sat at the table directly behind the box. Their job was to ensure that everyone who voted lived in the community and, therefore, had the right to place their ballot. Long lists of names and identification cards weren't needed in 1870; the men knew everyone who lived in the town—and if they missed someone, there were always townsfolk available to verify anyone's citizenship in the community.

With the name marked on her paper, Grandma Swain folded it lengthwise and then, just to be sure, folded it one more time along its width. When she was done, she got into the line of men waiting to place their papers into the locked wooden box. The line moved quickly and within minutes she had made it to the box. She smiled nervously at the two men as she moved her hand over to the long narrow opening. She took a deep breath and then slid her paper into the slot. The men smiled back and nodded. Grandma Swain walked away, a feeling of accomplishment sweeping over her. And so it was—with little fanfare—that on September 6, 1870, Eliza A. "Grandma" Swain became the first woman in America to vote in a public election.

While the first woman's vote may have been cast in 1870, the movement for the right of women to vote started long before that. In fact, it started almost twenty years earlier and half a country away, in 1852, with Susan B. Anthony and Elizabeth Cady Stanton in Rochester, New York. The two women had worked tirelessly to organize and garner support for the Republican Party, which was looking to pass the Thirteenth Amendment to the Constitution—an amendment that abolished slavery in the United States. Anthony and Stanton hoped the Republican Party would reward their support by, in turn, supporting the women's right to vote, known as suffrage. Unfortunately, the women would be disappointed when, after the amendment passed, that support failed to come.

Undaunted, in 1866 the two women organized a national movement called the American Equal Rights Association. Two years later they published a newspaper, which they named *The Revolution Rochester*. The paper came complete with a bold masthead that stated: "Men, their rights, and nothing more; women, their rights, and nothing less." Anthony and Stanton worked hard to campaign for a constitutional amendment, but the organization began to split and in 1869 an offshoot of their organization, called the American Woman Suffrage Association, was founded. Instead of trying to gain national support, this new organization decided to try a different strategy, one that concentrated on the individual states.

That same year, Esther Hobart Morris moved to a booming mining town in Wyoming called South Pass City. The Gold Rush of the late 1840s and early 1850s in California had come to a head, and in 1867 the discovery of gold in Wyoming's Rocky Mountains spawned the fast-growing town. In the summer of 1868 the Cariso Lode brought more than two thousand miners—and people looking to make money off of miners—to South Pass City. In 1869 Morris and her husband John caught gold fever and moved there to open a saloon.

Esther Hobart Morris's road to South Pass City was almost as rocky as the mountains she crossed to get there. Born on August 8, 1814, in Tioga County, New York, Morris became an orphan at only eleven years of age. She was taken in by a seamstress and hatmaker, who taught Morris the valuable skills she would use to run a successful business. It was while running that business in New York that Morris learned about social injustices among women and, because of that, joined the anti-slavery movement. During her time as a young businesswoman, Morris married, but in 1845 became a widow. She moved from New York to Peru, Illinois, to settle her husband's estate. It was while in Illinois that she married John Morris, himself a prosperous merchant. When opportunity knocked in Wyoming, the couple saw little choice but to answer.

The eastern part of the territory known as Wyoming had become part of the United States as a result of the Louisiana Purchase in 1803. Signed as a treaty with France, the Louisiana Purchase doubled the size of the United States. It also paved the way for the expansion of the west, which, as part of the agreement, was purchased for only four cents an acre. The remaining part of the territory came to be as a result of an 1846 land deal with Britain, called the Oregon Treaty, which resulted in the end of the Mexican War.

Frontier life was vastly different from life on the cultured east coast, especially for women. While learned men in the eastern states worried that women would be unable to fulfill their societal domestic roles if given equal rights, frontier women were already working hand-in-hand, pulling equal weight, with their male counterparts. In the frontier territory of Wyoming, it was the only way to survive.

Women in the territory of Wyoming were used to bucking the social norms of the 1800s. In fact, it was a theme consistent with Wyoming itself. In 1865 a Republican from Ohio, Representative James M. Ashley, presented a bill to establish a "temporary government for the territory of Wyoming." Ashley, who was the chairman of the Committee on Territories, was looking to help place the territory on its path to becoming a state. The bill never made it out of committee. This didn't stop the territory from establishing a government anyway. And when Congress finally passed the bill three years later, in 1868, the official territory of Wyoming elected its first official governor, John A. Campbell.

Almost immediately after moving to the small mining town of South Pass City, Esther Hobart Morris found a group of men and women interested in politics. These men and women attended tea parties hosted by Morris, who believed that giving women the right to vote would encourage families to settle in the newly established Wyoming territory. Morris believed so strongly in women's right to vote that she began lobbying the twenty-two members of the Wyoming legislature. One of those members was William H. Bright, who, at the urging of his wife Julia, introduced a bill at the territory's first legislative session giving women the right to vote. The bill passed, along with bills giving equal pay for female teachers, the right of women to serve on juries, and the right of married women to own property. When Governor Campbell signed the bill into law, the Equality State was born.

News of the vote spread rapidly, catching the attention of Susan B. Anthony, who immediately called for eastern women to move to the west. The recent completion of the transcontinental railroad brought tourists and journalists alike to the Wyoming Territory, all hoping to catch a glimpse of the wild liberties afforded to women in the west. As hundreds of people arrived to observe the culture of Wyoming, life went on for its residents, who seemed to take all the publicity—both good and bad—in stride. One time when the United States Congress threatened to delay Wyoming's passage as a state if they didn't refute women's suffrage, the territory answered sternly, stating that they would rather remain out of the union one hundred years than to join without women's suffrage.

Following their historic vote, Wyoming went on to elect Morris as the justice of the peace for the South Pass District on February 14, 1870. She served for eight and a half months and handled twenty-six cases. The next year three women were called to serve on juries. Through the next twenty years, Wyoming kept making its own rules and establishing its own path. Anthony continued promoting women's suffrage and in 1877 she managed to gather petitions from twenty-six states, amounting to more than ten thousand signatures, in support of the movement. Congress ignored the signatures. In 1887 the two existing women's suffrage organizations merged into the National American Woman Suffrage Association. Stanton was elected president and Anthony vice-president. A year later *Harper's Magazine* ran a story that described Wyoming women in the town of Cheyenne going door to door to register voters. In the article the women were dressed in their Sunday best as they politely performed their tasks.

That same year, in 1888, the Wyoming Territorial Assembly petitioned the United States Congress for statehood. The bill did not pass. Undaunted, the Wyoming Territory acted just as if it had passed. They organized a Constitutional Convention in September of 1889 and established a constitution, which was approved and voted into law two months later on November 5, 1889. Wyoming would have to wait until March 27, 1890 for President Benjamin Harrison to sign the bill admitting Wyoming into the union and making it the forty-fourth state.

When Wyoming entered the union, Morris was honored as a pioneer of women's suffrage. Five years later, in 1895, at the age of eighty, she was elected as a delegate to the national suffrage convention in Cleveland. Morris died in Cheyenne, Wyoming, on April 2, 1902, at the age of eighty-seven. Neither she nor Susan B. Anthony (who died on March 13, 1906) would live to see the passing of the Nineteenth Amendment to the Constitution granting all citizens of the United States—regardless of race or sex—the right to vote. The amendment was ratified on August 18, 1920. Four years later, Wyoming would again cast a historic vote and lead the nation by electing Nellie Tayloe Ross as the first female governor in the United States. While Anthony helped draft the amendment, it would take the United States thirty-two years to see the world through the eyes of the Wild West frontier territory that all along viewed women as equals.

THE JOHNSON COUNTY WAR

1892

They were surrounded. Twenty-five hired guns—invaders from Texas—were holed up at the T. A. Ranch just south of Buffalo, Wyoming, in the county of Johnson. Sometime in the night, close to two hundred men, mainly small-time ranchers, from the towns of Buffalo and Douglas had surrounded the T. A. The men were joined by a posse organized by Sheriff William "Red" Angus. The situation was dire. And if that wasn't bad enough, it was now snowing.

The invaders had fortified the ranch in anticipation of being besieged and now the time had come. Many of the men took cover in a barn on the property, a sixty- by forty-foot structure, constructed with one-inch-thick wooden walls. Because the barn had no windows, the invaders had to cut small holes in the north and south walls to use as gun ports. Others took refuge in the ranch house located next to the barn.

As the sun rose on April 11, 1892, the shooting started. The ranchers and posse took cover in the banks of the Crazy Woman Creek, which passed around the east side of the ranch, running north to south. The men shot at anything that moved. The invaders returned fire as they could, but both parties were essentially shooting blind. The men at the creek could not see those in the barn and the men in the barn were unable to get a good view of their attackers. They were also unwilling to waste ammunition. That concern did not plague the men at the creek, who kept up their fire almost continuously.

At one point one of the invaders tried to make a run for it. He was followed by several others who tried desperately to reach their corralled horses. Determined that no one was to escape, the posse opened fire on the men, concentrating their guns on the horses. After several of the horses fell, the escape attempt was abandoned and the men quickly returned to the barn.

The men at the creek used the confusion to fortify their position. They had circled the ranch and slowly began to tighten the circle, using bales of hay and whatever they could for cover. As they drew closer to the barn their shots became more accurate. They unleashed a barrage of gunfire, their bullets slamming through the walls of the barn, easily penetrating the thin wood. The men inside the barn were almost completely unable to return fire. All they could do was hunker down, taking occasional shots when breaks in the firing occurred.

The shooting continued throughout the day and, as night fell, desperation set in. One of the invaders volunteered to try to sneak out. He was given a hand-written note by another of the invaders—H. E. Teschemacher—with instructions to send the note as a telegraph to the governor of Wyoming. As the darkness set in, the volunteer—whose last name was Dowling—slipped out of the barn, crawling slowly on his belly. He managed to make his way to the creek, slipping down the bank and falling into the icy waters. He had barely made it to the other side of the bank when members of the posse came upon him. However, in the dark of night, Dowling was mistaken for a member of the posse and allowed to pass. He took a horse and headed into Buffalo. In the middle of the Johnson County war, one man had escaped and all hopes were now riding on him.

The Johnson County war began long before the shootout at T. A. Ranch. The Wyoming Territory in the late 1800s was a vast unsettled prairie. Massive herds of buffalo roamed freely across the territory, feeding on the rich short-grass prairie. Johnson County, Wyoming, was originally established by the territorial legislature in 1875 as Pease County, being named after Dr. E. L. Pease. Four years later the name was changed to Johnson County in honor of E. P. Johnson, US attorney for the Territory of Wyoming, who had recently passed.

In 1879, Johnson County was a one-hundred-by-one-hundred-square-mile patch of land that was bordered by Montana on the north, the Bighorn River in the Bighorn Basin on the west, and the Powder River on the east. It encompassed virtually the entire Bighorn Mountain chain, which gave the land an ample supply of water. Besides being rich in nutrients, the land was also almost completely unsettled.

A year earlier, in 1878, Captain Edwin Pollock of the Ninth US Cavalry was given orders to select a site for a fort along the Bozeman Trail. He chose an area in Pease County near Clear Creek where the stream first emerges out of the Bighorn Mountains. It would eventually become Fort McKinney. This opened the area to settlement, entrepreneurs, and opportunists. People came. According to T. V. McCandlish, editor of the *Buffalo Echo* (the first newspaper published in Johnson County), "On the banks of Clear Creek was soon gathered as rough an element of humanity as a frontier settlement is usually blessed or cursed with."

Along with the frontiersmen came the cattle. The area, being filled with rich, nourishing grass, was a perfect spot to raise cattle and, best of all, the land was free. The cattlemen came and with them herds filled with thousands of cattle. Because the area wasn't owned by any one person, the cattlemen let their cattle roam the plains, grazing on the rich prairie grass—which cost them nothing. Their herds, being fed well, increased and by 1880 the cattlemen had become very wealthy. They went from cattlemen to cattle barons, resembling the lords of England.

The barons formed an organization known as the Wyoming Stockmen's Association. They summered in Cheyenne, Wyoming, where they built a meeting place called the Cheyenne Club. The male-only club was lavishly furnished. It was the place to see and be seen. Cattle barons mingled with wealthy businessmen, high-ranking professionals, and, most importantly, state and federal legislators. The cattle barons, or more appropriately, the cattle barons' money, influenced everything, and their power was far reaching, but not so far as to be able to stop progress.

Almost twenty years earlier, on May 20, 1862, President Abraham Lincoln had signed into law the Homestead Act, opening millions of acres of the public domain to settlement and cultivation. The act brought people by the thousands to the West, many of whom began to claim the land used by the cattle barons for grazing. The settlers fenced off their lands and the cattle barons could only watch as their precious prairie began to get smaller and smaller. In desperation they tried to fight back. They destroyed fences and left menacing notes on the homes of the settlers. They even tried to buy the settlers out. When all their efforts failed, they accused many of the new settlers of rustling their cows—an act that had probably taken place, but was typically overlooked. In a final act of desperation, they hired twenty-five gunmen, who came to be called "invaders," from Texas to hunt down and kill several small-time ranchers the cattle barons had targeted for extermination. Two of those ranchers had already been killed when the men reached the T. A. Ranch.

The ranch was owned by Dr. William Harris of Laramie. Harris had purchased the brand and herd from Tom Alsop, the T. A. of T. A. Ranch. Harris moved the herd to Johnson County and hired Charles Ford as manager, so he could remain in Laramie to practice medicine. Harris was politically aligned with the Wyoming Stockmen's Association and it was for that reason the invaders chose to seek shelter at the T. A. Ranch.

At the ranch on the night of April 11, bullets continued to fly. Some of the invaders took shelter in the ranch house while others chose the barn. One of the invaders holed up in the house, a man by the name of Billy Irvine, told fellow invader H. E. Teschemacher to move away from the window. He did so and moments later a bullet came crashing through that same window. All around them bullets crashed through the windows of the ranch house and penetrated the walls of the barn, so much so that the invaders hardly dared walk upright. The men on the ranch had limited ammunition and limited resources. Food was scarce and supplies even more so. On the other hand, the men surrounding the ranch had plenty of supplies and could rotate men from the front lines as necessary.

Dowling, the invader who escaped, had made it to the telegraph and had gotten a message to Acting Governor Amos W. Barber. Barber was a supporter of the cattle barons. He knew of the invasion and had cleared the way for the hired gunmen to proceed unimpeded by ordering the state militia not to get involved with the local sheriffs.

On April 12, 1892, reinforcements came for the men at the river, increasing their numbers. Just as the situation seemed hopeless, Governor Barber stepped in. He sent a telegraph to President Benjamin Harrison stating, "An insurrection exists in Johnson County, in the State of Wyoming, in the immediate vicinity of Fort McKinney, against the government of said state." Barber neglected to provide the president any details regarding how the insurrection started or the cattle barons' involvement in the incident. With the help of two Wyoming senators, Joseph M. Carey and Francis E. Warren, Barber finally got a hold of the president. Harrison sent in troops "to protect the state of Wyoming against domestic violence."

Within two hours, troops from nearby Fort McKinney were dispatched to the T. A. Ranch. They arrived the next day, on April 13, 1892, and rescued the invaders without incident. The men and posse at the river watched helplessly as the troops took the invaders (also called regulators) into custody. The invaders were all brought up on charges for the killing of one of the two ranchers (Nate Champion), sparking a newspaper skirmish as the papers aligned with the cattle barons battled against the papers not under their influence. The battle raged on and in the process the invaders, who came from Texas, were freed on forty thousand dollars' bail. Once released they immediately fled to Texas. None of the men were ever convicted.

The cattle barons had become so powerful that they deemed themselves beyond the reach of everyone, including the law. They tried to take over a territory known for being wild and in turn found that its residents could only be pushed so far. The cattle barons were through. They couldn't fight progress and they couldn't tame Wyoming.

YELLOWSTONE NATIONAL PARK

EMMA COWAN AND THE NEZ PERCE

1877

So far, the Cowans' trip through Yellowstone National Park had been wonderful. They'd seen the geysers and the paint pots, then climbed into the Grand Canyon of the Yellowstone River. Tonight they should have been in high spirits, planning to break camp and head home the next day with a lifetime full of happy memories and wondrous stories to tell of the sights they'd seen during their summer vacation in "Wonderland." The men pulled out a violin and guitar and began to play and sing while Emma Cowan and her twelve-year-old sister Ida Carpenter clapped and listened, though they didn't feel as merry as they might have. Earlier that day, they had been warned by General Sherman, who was passing through the area, that the Nez Perce Indians had just been in a battle with the US Army at Big Hole, in Idaho, and were thought to be on their way north into Montana, perhaps even passing near the park.

Emma Cowan had come to Montana Territory as a ten-year-old with her pioneering family. They lived in Virginia City, and from her childhood Emma remembered the tales told of the Yellowstone area by an old trapper who lived there. Though many people disregarded his fantastic tales of the sights to be seen, Emma was still anxious to visit the area and did so in 1873 for the first time, just after the area was designated as the world's first national park.

The summer of 1877 was a hot and dry one in Montana Territory, and Emma and her husband George required little convincing to close up their house against encroaching mosquitoes for the cooler altitude of Yellowstone when Emma's brother, Frank Carpenter, suggested it. On August 6, the party set out from Radersburg, Montana, with nine people. They were handsomely outfitted with a double-seated carriage, a wagon to carry their supplies, and four saddle horses, including Emma's own pony.

As they headed into the park along the Madison River from the northwest, they heard rumors that there was likely to be trouble in the area from the Nez Perce tribe of Idaho. They disregarded the stories and were quickly so busy enjoying the cool air, beautiful flowers, tasty wildlife, and solitude, that they thought nothing more of it until August 23, after they'd explored nearly all of the sites of Yellowstone, when they met with General Sherman's party, which was looking for the Nez Perce.

As they sat by the fire on that same night, enjoying the antics of the men, Emma Cowan and her sister didn't know that carefully concealed in the shadows beyond their camp circle was a band of fleeing Nez Perce Indians who had just entered the park in their search for refuge from the pursuing US Army.

The Nez Perce conflict, like so many other conflicts between the United States government and the native peoples of the United States territories, was triggered by an argument about land. For generations, the Nez Perce had peacefully occupied the Wallowa Valley in northeastern Oregon. Since their first encounters with the Lewis and Clark Expedition in 1805, they had prided themselves on never killing a white man.

In 1855, the Nez Perce ceded part of their land to the US government and accepted life on a reservation in their homeland. In 1863, after the discovery of gold in the area, the government asked for more of the Nez Perce's land and part of the tribe agreed. The other part remained where they were, however, in spite of encroaching settlement by whites, and in 1873, President Ulysses S. Grant signed an executive order that guaranteed the territory to the Nez Perce, invalidating the 1863 treaty. The white settlers continued making trouble, however, and refused to leave their claims. Eventually, in 1875, President Grant rescinded his earlier order under intense pressure. Even after a young Nez Perce leader named Chief Joseph tried to negotiate a settlement with the government the verdict was the same—the Nez Perce were told to vacate the Wallowa by April 1877. The timing would force them to make all of their preparations in the dead of winter and would give them only thirty days to accomplish what in practical terms should have taken up to six months. Many Nez Perce urged Chief Joseph to go to war against the US government so they would not have to leave their homes.

Chief Joseph refused, and as the plans for the move continued, frustration mounted among the Nez Perce. Finally, a small group of renegade Nez Perce went on a raiding party in Chief Joseph's absence and killed more than twenty white men.

When the US Army heard news of the raids, the cavalry was sent in to forcibly escort the Nez Perce to the reservation. By that time, Joseph felt that the use of force was unavoidable, and a battle ensued where the cavalry was severely routed and the Nez Perce began a retreat toward the Bitterroot Valley of southwestern Montana Territory. From there, they formed a plan to go to Canada. A reinforced army met them at Clearwater on July 11, where after another battle they headed across the mountains, through Lolo Pass, and into Montana Territory. They then turned south, and on August 9, the army made a surprise attack against their camp in the Big Hole. Losses were great on both sides, but again the Nez Perce escaped. This time, they headed toward Yellowstone National Park, and after another altercation on August 20, found themselves near the Cowans' exploring camp in the Lower Geyser Basin.

Upon awaking on the morning of August 24, Emma Cowan found twenty to thirty Nez Perce in the Cowans' camp, demanding supplies.

George Cowan refused to allow their looting, and for a while it still seemed that the party of vacationers would be allowed to pack up their belongings and leave the park unmolested. However, not long after the party had moved out, they were required by the Nez Perce to backtrack to a place where they had to abandon their carriage and wagon. They were allowed a few meager possessions, and then their supplies were looted and ransacked. The Nez Perce were extremely well armed, and the Cowans were not since they had used most of their ammunition for hunting during the trip.

Later that day, the Nez Perce forced them to give up their mounts in exchange for other horses that could barely walk, though again they were promised that they could leave peacefully on them. But again the Cowan party was called back to the camp almost as soon as they had left. This time, however, there was to be more trouble. Suddenly shots rang out and Emma Cowan found herself crouched with her young sister near her husband, who had been shot from his horse. While they cowered there, a Nez Perce roughly grabbed Emma and pulled her aside, pointed his gun at her husband's head, and shot him again. The rest of the party was taken hostage and George Cowan's body was left where he fell.

After a long night, the party was again given horses and told they could leave. This time, they were allowed to reach the safety of Mammoth Hot Springs, where a grieving Emma was escorted home.

After a week in safety, she heard the unbelievable news that her husband was still alive. Another week later it was confirmed that he would be arriving in Bozeman, Montana, and she rushed there to find that he had made it no farther than the Bottler Ranch, a common stopping place for visitors on the road between Bozeman and the park. She met him there, and though she found him in serious condition, he was anxious and able to travel home with her.

The ending of the story was not as kind to the Nez Perce. After two more battles with the army on their flight to Canada, they were kept in a state of siege in the Bears Paw Mountains in northern Montana as the bitter winds of October blew in. Finally, Chief Joseph surrendered his people with one of the most eloquent speeches in history. It ended,

> *It is cold and we have no blankets. The little children are freezing to death. . . . I want to have time to look for my children and see how many I can find. Maybe I shall find them among the dead. Hear me, my chiefs. I am tired; my heart is sick and sad. From where the sun now stands, I will fight no more forever.*

Emma Cowan later recalled her harrowing experience eloquently as well, and with no malice in her heart. She relished the memory of playing, singing, and dancing on carefree nights in the park, and when she looked back on the events that transpired in the following days and weeks she bore no ill will toward her captors and her husband's would-be murderers. Though her pleasure trip to Yellowstone had been marred, the memory of it did not linger as a nightmare but as a dream of times past and merrymaking. She later said of the Nez Perces taking their horses,

> *It occurs to me at this writing, that the above mode of trading is a fair reflection of the lesson taught by the whites. For instance, a tribe of Indians are located on a reservation. Gold is discovered thereon by some prospector. A stampede follows. The strong arm of the government alone prevents the avaricious pale face from possessing himself of the land forthwith. Soon negotiations are pending with as little delay as a few yards of red tape will admit. A treaty is signed, the strip ceded to the government and opened to settlers, and "Lo, the poor Indian" finds himself on a tract a few degrees more arid, a little less desirable than his former home.*

But her most eloquent reflection on the Nez Perce incident was this:

Yet, at this day, knowing something of the circumstances that led to the final outbreak and uprising of these Indians, I wonder that any of us were spared. Truly a quality of mercy was shown us during our captivity that a Christian might emulate, and at a time when they must have hated the very name of the white race.

THE LEWIS
AND CLARK
EXPEDITION

GRIZZLY ENCOUNTERS

1805

Captain Lewis walked along the shore—as he often did, preferring steady ground beneath his feet to the motion of the small boats in the rushing river—recording the number of animals and beauty of the landscape around them. After a long, cold winter with the Mandans at the fort on the Missouri, the crisp breezes of spring were a delight to the men as they made their way west.

The animals were abundant, and the species diverse. Elk, bison, pronghorn, deer, wolves, and grizzly bears dotted the landscape on either side of the river. Other than Pierre Cruzatte's brief encounter with the grizzly that he wounded the previous fall, the expedition had yet to experience the great bear other than through the reports of others and the claws they'd seen hanging long and menacing on the necklaces of Native Americans they'd met on the way. Paw prints proved the size of these animals, but they had yet to kill one.

Bears were a valuable commodity—in addition to the large quantity of meat, they also produced oil from their fat, and the hides were extremely thick and durable—but the expedition must also have been interested in them as a species, and interested in vanquishing one just to see if they could do it. Grizzly bears were unknown in the East.

Lewis reported of his journey on shore on April 29.

> *I walked on shore with one man. about 8. a.m. we fell in with two brown or yellow bear; both of which we wounded; one of them made his escape, the other after my firing on him pursued me seventy or eighty yards, but fortunately had been so badly wounded that he was unable to pursue me so closely as to prevent my charging my gun; we again repeated our fire and killed him. it was a male not fully grown, we estimated his weight at 300 lbs. not having the means of ascertaining it precisely. The legs of this bear are somewhat longer than those of the black, as are it's tallons and tusks incomparably larger and longer.*

It was the first grizzly kill of the expedition, a small bear that Lewis examined closely and reported on in detail, ending his account with the comment, "in the hands of skillfull riflemen they are by no means as formidable or dangerous as they have been represented."

Lewis would change his opinion. Over the next few days, they saw grizzlies everywhere. And their success in dealing with them was mixed. Six days later, Clark went out with George Drouillard, and it took ten bullets to kill a bear that was "the largest of the carnivorous kind I ever saw."

In his measurements of that bear, Lewis reported, "it was a most tremendious looking animal, and extremely hard to kill notwithstanding he had five balls through his lungs and five others in various parts he swam more than half the distance across the river to a sandbar, & it was at least twenty minutes before he died."

The experience with the bears was impressive. A few days later, when one of the party wounded a bear on his own, he did not pursue it to the end of the battle. The bears had won the respect of even the rifle-wielding mountain men.

THE OREGON
TRAIL

THE LAST GREAT CHALLENGE
The Barlow Road

1853

Amelia Stewart Knight stood ankle deep in the fine prairie sand on the barren Nebraska plains. The heartless winds whipped dust mercilessly about, sparing no one its cruel bite. Amelia tugged the brim of her bonnet with both hands to shield her face and pondered what to serve for breakfast. Today there would be no morning fire to cook a hearty meal. Instead the fare would consist of leftover bacon, hard biscuits, and day-old, cold coffee. Amelia told her seven children, huddled against each other for protection against the cloud of dust, to eat hurriedly. Her journal entry for Friday, May 13, 1853, read, "Them that eat the most breakfast eat the most sand."

Relief was not in sight until the cool rains came, the winds died down, and the dust was finally tamed. There were to be countless vexations like this one on their five-month journey from Monroe County, Iowa, clear to the Willamette Valley in far-off Oregon. None would compare, however, to the nearly insurmountable obstacle near trail's end that the Knight family encountered months later.

Boston-born Amelia Stewart married Joel Knight when she was seventeen. After living in Boston for three years, Joel moved his family to Monroe County, Iowa. Sixteen years later Joel caught the "Oregon Fever" and decided to leave Iowa and join the throngs of westbound emigrants. Oregon's lush Willamette Valley, oft written about in the newspapers, promised the opportunity for a better life and was perhaps the ideal location to practice his medicine. So the Knights packed up their seven children, ranging in age from two to seventeen, into three covered wagons and set out to cross the plains. Amelia, ever-optimistic, was up for the challenge—if only the nagging illness she felt would go away.

The early part of their journey was plagued by alternating storms of rain, dust, and hail. In their zeal to beat the winter snows and cross the mountains to Oregon, the Knights left the second week of April. The early start caused delays as the oxen and wagon wheels got mired in the muddy prairie soil from the spring rains. Violent thunderstorms with lightning-pierced skies sent the livestock stampeding, sending the rain-drenched men out to round up oxen and cattle. Amelia recorded in her journal, "The men and boys are all soaking wet and look sad and comfortless. The little ones and myself are shut up in the wagons from the rain . . . every body out of humour."

The rains chased them out of Nebraska into Wyoming. Temperatures ranged from 110 degrees in desert crossings to 30 degrees and frozen ground. Joel Knight had hired five hands to help get his family to Oregon, yet halfway through the journey only two remained up to the challenge. Though often not feeling well herself, Amelia nursed her husband and children through fevers, mumps, poison ivy outbreaks, scarlet fever, and mosquito attacks. One of Amelia's younger daughters was traumatically left behind the caravan and temporarily lost. Her two-year-old son fell out of the covered wagon twice, narrowly missing being run over by the wagon wheels bearing twenty-five hundred pounds of provisions.

It was a rough ride "jumping and jolting over rocks all day" at the base of mountain cliffs. Amelia climbed down six feet of slippery rock to ford river crossings with six children in tow. Mustering the energy to hike back up to the other side sapped her strength. The stench of the rotting carrion from oxen and cattle dropping dead in their tracks along the trail was especially hard to stomach.

As they began the ascent of the mountains into Oregon, everyone's spirits picked up—only to be tested to the limit less than three weeks later. Amelia rested two or three times as she climbed the steep hills with her children, often carrying her two-year-old son. But the hills were just a precursor to the trail's greatest challenge. Looming before them on September 8 was the highest point of the Cascade Range: 11,235-foot Mount Hood. The emigrants needed to bypass this giant obstacle to reach the much-sought-after Willamette Valley. There were only two choices: They could either raft down the raging Columbia River or go through the heavily wooded forest on Mount Hood.

Though the Oregon Trail ended at The Dalles, a place of rocky river rapids on the Columbia River, the Knights' destination was beyond that in Oregon City in the Willamette Valley. The decision to build rafts and go down the raging river's ruthless currents, foaming crests, and hidden whirlpools cost many emigrants their lives. As the wild Columbia River passed through the narrow gorge, it gained momentum before forcefully continuing on its way. The Knights considered building their own crude rafts, but that would take time, and time was exactly what they did not have. They could pay an outrageous fee of fifty to one hundred dollars to raft downriver or trade their prized livestock to ferry across. But even hiring experienced Indian boatmen did not guarantee safe passage. The Knights opted to take the land route, which required a lesser toll of five dollars for each wagon and ten cents per head of livestock.

Lucky for them, a path called the Barlow Road had opened on the southern slope of Mount Hood seven years earlier. The Oregon provincial legislature was well aware of the difficulty emigrants faced entering Oregon due to Mount Hood blocking their way. Samuel K. Barlow was granted permission to collect tolls if he would clear a path through the mountains, allowing for the passage of covered wagons. Barlow and Joel Palmer forged an overland route in 1845 by hacking down tree after tree. The Barlow Road opened by 1846, when approximately one thousand people and 145 wagons made it through. Grateful for not having to clear the path themselves, emigrants endured traveling a road that was still primitive and proved to be the single most difficult challenge along the Oregon Trail. The ninety-mile Barlow Road reached an elevation of 4,155 feet.

Portions of the Barlow Road seemed downright intolerable. On the road's infamous Laurel Hill, the men used ropes and chains tied around trees to winch their wagons downhill, placing logs in front of the wheels to slow the descent. They also put logs through the rear wheels or tied logs to the rear axles to act as brakes to prevent the wagons from tumbling down the mountain. Unable to help, Amelia watched as man and beast heaved and hoisted the wagons to the point of exhaustion and collapse. Laurel Hill was a series of three declines, the worst being a 60 percent grade.

For fourteen miles they traveled up and down over the hellacious rock- and stump-strewn hill. The roughest patch was composed of twisting exposed tree roots, fallen logs, and mud holes. The Knights wound their way around decapitated tree stumps and fallen trees. Their wagon wheels creaked and jerked over the rough undergrowth and sunk into deep trenches with a harsh jarring motion. The provisions inside their wagon clanged against each other, running the risk of being catapulted up and over the sides.

There was no side path to avoid the timber and fallen trees through the mountains of dense forest of Ponderosa pines and Douglas firs. Amelia looked up past the three-hundred-foot-tall trees of the canopied forest and must have wondered if the road could not have been cleared a little better. The rope-worn stumps were evidence of wagons before them being inched down Laurel Hill. The road was strewn with abandoned trunks, barrels, and possessions too heavy to be hoisted down the steep slopes. Sitting at the very bottom of the hill were the remains of wagons that had slipped and crashed. Amelia's heart went out to the fatigued oxen that, forced to go just one more mile, had collapsed under the strain and were left dead in their yokes on the sides of the road. Yet the Barlow Road was not done testing the Knights' mettle.

Two phenomenally trying days later, Amelia recorded in her journal, "It would be useless for me with my pencil to describe the awful road we have just passed over (let fancy picture a train of wagons and cattle passing through a crooked chimney and we have Big Laurel Hill). After descending several bad hills, one called Little Laurel Hill, which I thought is as bad as could be, but in reality it was nothing to this last one called Big Laurel."

Big Laurel Hill was more than a half mile long and just like Little Laurel Hill, except worse in every regard. The steep, rocky, winding grade was strewn with obstacles, both natural and man-made. A small spring ran the length of the hill, making for a sloppy, slippery death trap. Joel Knight and the other men and boys inched their wagons down by securing ropes and chains around stumps. The nearly vertical descent seemed impossible. To add to their stress, an emigrant's wagon directly in front of them kept stopping, while behind them was another wagon whose men cursed at them in their frustration with the delays. All the while Amelia and her children painstakingly sidestepped their way down to prevent from tumbling. She carried her youngest in her arms on the dangerous descent as they crawled over a sea of fallen timber, finally arriving safely at the bottom of Big Laurel Hill.

It is no wonder Amelia Stewart Knight found the westward trek, especially the Barlow Road and Laurel Hill, challenging. Less than two weeks later, her "nagging illness" revealed itself and she delivered her eighth, but not last, child, a son. With a newborn in tow, Amelia and her seven other children and husband made the last leg of their journey by water. They traveled by skiff, canoe, and flatboat for three days on the Columbia River to the mouth of the Willamette River, then upriver to Oregon City, their final destination. Joel Knight traded his oxen for a half section of land partially planted, and they all moved into a small cabin and lean-to with no windows, happy to have beaten the winter snows. Amelia, surely exhausted beyond comprehension, wrote her last entry in her journal, flatly stating, "This is the journey's end."

THE SANTA
FE TRAIL

A WINTER CROSSING
OF THE PRAIRIE

1852

The old-timers at Independence shook their heads. A mere eighteen men, three wagons, and three carriages—with three women and two children—were going to brave the plains? The caravan was not large enough to fend off an attack. But even worse was the month—October. It was madness. They would all be lost.

But Dr. Michael Steck did not listen. He had been appointed as agent for the Mescalero Apaches in New Mexico. Duty called, and he proposed to go. The first couple of days on the trail were great fun. Dr. Michael shot prairie chickens and personally supervised their cooking. Then it began to rain. And it rained, all the way to Council Grove, where they arrived in about a week.

The Kanza Indian agency was situated at Council Grove, and at this time of year, the tribe drew annual rations. The Kanza performed the buffalo dance, which amused Dr. Michael and company. But the festivities soon turned dark when some young men arrived, riding dramatically through the mud streets of the prairie village. On a lance one carried the scalp of their foe, a Shawnee, making for great excitement and cheering on the part of the Indians, and a scalp dance was performed.

The next day Dr. Michael and his party left Council Grove, happy to be away from the "civilized" Kanza Indians. That afternoon in the hills west of the village, a prairie thunderstorm caught them. Bolts of lightning electrified the gloomy afternoon. Peals of thunder echoed off the hills and rolled down the valleys as buckets of water cascaded out of the sky. The mules had better sense than their drivers. They refused to go on, turning their rumps into the storm. The humans huddled in their carriages and wagons, eating cold meat and hardtack for supper. By nightfall the wind dropped, and they pitched tents. Though there was no wood for a fire to warm them, they slept soundly. The next day, though still traveling in rain, they headed for the next good camping spot, Cottonwood Creek, twenty miles away. The trail had been churned to peanut butter by the rains, but they slogged on. Dark came, and every lurch threatened to dump a vehicle into a gully. They kept on, arriving at the creek about eight in the evening. After chores, which included picketing the animals, gathering firewood, and cooking supper, a meal was ready to eat by eleven at night.

All this called for a little rest and some thanksgiving. Ducks and turkeys were shot and roasted. The following day Dr. Michael and company trekked to Big Turkey Creek. Dr. Michael sensed danger. A spot was seen moving on the prairie, soon identified as an Indian. Since they were still in Osage territory, an attack was unlikely, but the theft of their mules was possible. In such situations the Osage usually pretended to have found "strayed" animals and offered to give them back—for a reward. But the men took no chances. They were on the edge of the plains. The loss of the animals, especially with winter approaching, could be disastrous. They posted a double guard.

Dr. Michael had been right in his belief danger was at hand. But it didn't come from the Indians. The next afternoon it began to snow. This was not the puffy, white, Christmas kind of snowfalls he had come to expect in Pennsylvania. This was a plains snowstorm with strong winds. They were on the high prairie with not a stick of wood in sight. Four inches of snow was on the ground and the trail ruts were filling. When the ruts were completely obscured, they'd be lost. Then suddenly, as all hope seemed lost, the sun came out. It quit snowing, and before them was the Little Arkansas with plentiful wood and a good camping spot. Disaster had been averted.

They pressed on. Now it was very cold, but that slight inconvenience was made up for by entering the buffalo range. Fresh meat was at hand. That was good. Not so good was the band of forty-five Osage hunters they encountered. As allies of the white man, the Osage crowded into camp and pressed the demands of friendship. Dr. Michael was afraid their mules were about to be stolen. Then worse, ahead more men on horseback were spotted. But these turned out to be a company of dragoons from Fort Atkinson (near present-day Dodge City). The Indians left, but now another storm threatened. However, this time the travelers knew what to do. Some gathered wood, others picketed the animals in sheltered locations, and yet others reinforced the tent ropes.

The next morning, despite the storm, they were up early. They trekked along the Arkansas River. It continued being excessively cold. Buffalo were everywhere, and so were wolves. Sometimes as many as fifty wolves would be seen at the same time. Whenever one pressed too close to the caravan, it would be shot. On the fourth day they reached Fort Atkinson. Because of the women and children in the party, the officers treated them kindly, but after two days Dr. Michael resumed his march along the river. Snow on the upland prairie drove the buffalo down along the river. It seemed as though the vast buffalo herd had to be parted to allow passage of the small wagon train.

Quicksand bogged down one of the wagons a hundred yards from shore when they were crossing the Arkansas. They had to wade the river in the freezing cold, unloading the contents by hand. Finally, the wagon was extracted, and they headed southwest across the Cimarron Desert.

Dr. Michael's band made twenty-two miles to Bear Creek. Digging in the bed of the creek did not produce water. They were by no means sure any would be found the next day either, when someone remembered spying a snow bank a few miles back, and men were sent to retrieve some snow. Just enough fuel was found to melt the water. Everyone received a cup of coffee and the animals were given a quart of water apiece.

The night was dark and stormy. As it progressed, snow began to fall and it became much, much colder. The mules, on their picket ropes, started shivering. That was a bad sign. The Cimarron Desert was known for terrible blizzards that killed stock. A trader by the name of Albert Speyer had lost 175 animals not far from that very spot just five years before. The skulls of the animals could still be seen on the side of the trail. The men unrolled themselves from their blankets and took their covers and wrapped them around the animals.

Returning to the tent, they amused themselves with stories of freighters lost in blizzards on the plains. One of them told about the wagon train that lost two hundred mules just the winter before and described how two of the men who tried to walk out froze to death. About two o'clock in the morning, the snow on the tent became too heavy. The guy ropes pulled out and the frozen fabric collapsed on those inside. The folks had a good laugh about this. They decided to leave the tent as it was. The snow acted as insulation, and so while others talked, Dr. Michael thought back to the delicacy one of the old trappers with them had cooked up a few days before. He had taken a buffalo calf's head, dug a hole, placed rocks in the bottom, and then poured coals from a fire on top. The calf's head was placed in the hole. More coals were added and the hole was covered. Breakfast the next morning was an untold delight, baked calf's head. Clearly, the men (and women and children) who braved the Santa Fe Trail were hardy and adventurous folk.

Dr. Michael and his family defied initial expectations and succeeded in their crossing of the plains. Once safely ensconced in New Mexico, Dr. Michael found the job as Indian agent immensely satisfying—and the Mescalero Apache thought he was a good agent. During the Civil War, when military rule was the order of the day, Dr. Steck stood up for the Indians, earning the condemnation of many whites but the gratitude of his Apache wards. Much later, long after the Civil War, he returned to Pennsylvania and spent his last days in the state of his youth.

BIBLIOGRAPHY

ALASKA

Adventure on Ice

Muir, John. *Stickeen: The Story of a Dog.* 1909. Reprint, Garden City, NY: Doubleday and Company, 1974.

Sherwood, Morgan B. *Exploration of Alaska: 1865–1900.* New Haven, CT: Yale University Press, 1965.

Young, S. Hall. *Alaska Days with John Muir.* New York: Fleming H. Revell Company, 1915.

Death on the Glacier

Barry, Mary J. *A History of Mining on the Kenai Peninsula, Alaska.* Anchorage: MJP Barry, 1997.

ARIZONA

The Ordeal of the Oatman Girls

Stratton, Royal B. *Life Among the Indians: Being an Interesting Narrative of the Captivity of the Oatman Girls.* San Francisco: Whitton, Towne & Co's Excelsior Steam Power Presses, 1857. Reprinted several times as *Captivity of the Oatman Girls.*

The Brief Success of the Overland Mail

Conkling, Roscoe P., and Margaret B. Conkling. *The Butterfield Overland Mail 1857–1869.* Glendale, CA: The Arthur H. Clark Company, 1947.

GRAND CANYON

The Cruel Colorado

Smith, Dwight L., ed. *The Photographer and the River, 1889–1890: The Colorado Cañon Diary of Franklin A. Nims with the Brown-Stanton Railroad Survey Expedition.* Santa Fe: Stagecoach Press, 1967.

Smith, Dwight L., and C. Gregory Compton. *The Colorado River Survey: Robert B. Stanton and the Denver, Colorado & Pacific Railroad.* Salt Lake City: Howe Brothers, 1987.

Stanton, Robert Brewster. *Colorado River Controversies.* 1932. Reprint, Boulder City, NE: Westwater Books, 1982.

———. *Down the Colorado.* Norman, Okla.: University of Oklahoma Press, 1965.

———. "Through the Grand Cañon of the Colorado." *Scribner's Magazine* 8 (November 1890): 591–613.

NORTHERN CALIFORNIA

Gold from the American River!
and The Head of Joaquin Murieta

Hart, James D. *Companion to California.* Berkeley: University of California Press, 1987.

Hutchinson, W. H. *California: Two Centuries of Man, Land, and Growth in the Golden State.* Palo Alto, CA: American West Publishing Co., 1969.

SAN FRANCISCO

Hallidie's Hill Climber

Bacon, Daniel. "Riding and Remembering the Cable Cars of San Francisco with Daniel Bacon." *Hemispheres,* March 1996,

Bunnell, J. S. "Towed by Rail." *St. Nicholas Magazine,* November 1878.

Hallidie, A. S. "The Wire Rope Railways of San Francisco, California." *Scientific American Supplement*, September 17, 1881.

Joe Thompson's Cable Car Guy website: www.cable-car-guy.com.

Svanevik, Michael, and Shirley Burgett. "How Hallidie's Invention Reshaped the Map of the City." *San Francisco Examiner*, October 14, 2001.

YOSEMITE NATIONAL PARK

Waterfall on Fire

Demars, Stanford E. *The Tourist in Yosemite 1855–1985.* Salt Lake City: University of Utah Press, 1991.

Sanborn, Margaret. *Yosemite: Its Discovery, Its Wonders and Its People.* New York: Random House, 1981.

Taylor, Katherine Ames. *Yosemite Tales and Trails.* Sacramento, CA: H. S. Crocker Co., Inc., 1934.

SOUTHERN CALIFORNIA

An Atmosphere of Suspicion

Cho, Jenny. *Chinatown in Los Angeles.* Los Angeles: Arcadia Publishing, 2009.

Goldberg, George. *East Meets West: The Story of the Chinese and Japanese in California.* New York: Harcourt Brace Jovanovich, 1970.

A Day of Rest

Caughey, John, and LaRee Caughey. *Los Angeles: Biography of a City.* Berkeley: University of California Press, 1976.

Dinkelspiel, Frances. *Towers of Gold: How One Jewish Immigrant Named Isaac Hellman Created California.* New York: St. Martin's Press, 2008.

Vorspan, Max, and Lloyd P. Gartner. *History of the Jews of Los Angeles.* San Marino, CA: Huntington Library, 1970.

COLORADO

The Blazing of the Goodnight-Loving Trail

Haley, J. Evetts. "Charles Goodnight, Pioneer." *Panhandle-Plains Historical Review,* Vol. 3, 1930.

The Great Diamond Hoax

Lamar, Howard R., ed. "The Great Diamond Hoax," *The Reader's Encyclopedia of the American West.* New York: Harper & Row, 1977.

DENVER

The Great Flood

Brenneman, Bill. *Miracle on Cherry Creek; An Informal History of the Birth and Re-Birth of a Neighborhood.* Denver: World Press, Inc., 1973.

Dorsett, Lyle W., and Michael McCarthy. *The Queen City: A History of Denver.* Boulder, CO: Pruett Publishing Company, 1986.

Etter, Don D. *Auraria: Where Denver Began.* Boulder: Colorado Associated University Press, 1972.

ROCKY MOUNTAIN NATIONAL PARK

The First Recorded Ascent of Longs Peak

Arps, Louisa Ward, and Elinor Eppich Kingery. *High Country Names: Rocky Mountain National Park and Indian Peaks.* Boulder, CO: Johnson Books, 1994.

Buchholtz, Curt W. *Rocky Mountain National Park: A History.* Boulder: Colorado Associated University Press, 1983.

Bueler, William M. *Roof of the Rockies: A History of Mountaineering in Colorado.* Boulder, CO: Pruett Publishing Co., 1974.

Byers, William N. "Ascent of Longs Peak." *Rocky Mountain News,* September 21, 1864; September 23, 1864.

Pickering, James H. *Early Estes Park Narratives.* Vol. 4. Estes Park, CO: Alpenaire Publishing, 2004.

Willard, Beatrice Elizabeth, and Susan Quimby Foster. *A Roadside Guide to Rocky Mountain National Park.* Boulder, CO: Johnson Books, 1990.

IDAHO

The Test Oath

Colson, Dennis C. *Idaho's Constitution: The Tie That Binds.* Moscow: University of Idaho Press, 1991.

Wells, Merle. *Anti-Mormonism in Idaho, 1872–92.* Provo, UT: Brigham Young University Press, 1978.

KANSAS

The Pottawatomie Massacre

"John Brown's Holy War," PBS, producer Robbie Kenner, 1999.

Townsley, James. "The Pottawatomie Killings." *Republican Citizen,* December 20, 1879, p. 5.

Exodusters

Hamilton, Kenneth Marvin. "The Origins and Early Promotion of Nicodemus: A Pre-Exodus, All-Black Town." *Kansas History,* 5, no. 4 (Winter 1982): 220–42.

Miner, Craig. *West of Wichita: Settling the High Plains of Kansas, 1865–1890.* Lawrence: The University Press of Kansas, 1986.

MISSOURI

The New Madrid Earthquake

Foley, William. *The Genesis of Missouri: From Wilderness Outpost to Statehood.* Columbia: University of Missouri Press, 1989.

————. *A History of Missouri. Vol. I: 1673 to 1820.* Columbia: University of Missouri Press, 1971.

Parrish, William, Charles Jones Jr., and Lawrence Christensen. *Missouri: The Heart of the Nation.* 3rd ed. Wheeling, IL: Harlan Davidson, 2004.

Sampson, Francis. "The New Madrid and Other Earthquakes in Missouri." *Missouri Historical Review* 92, no. 3 (April 1998).

A Slave Sues for His Freedom

Finkelman, Paul. *Dred Scott vs. Sandford: A Brief History with Documents.* Boston: Bedford Books, 1997.

Greene, Lorenzo J., et al. *Missouri's Black Heritage.* St. Louis: Forum Press, 1980.

McCandless, Perry. *A History of Missouri. Volume II: 1820 to 1860.* Columbia: University of Missouri Press, 1972.

Merkel, Benjamin. "The Abolition Aspects of Missouri's Antislavery Controversy, 1819–1865." *Missouri Historical Review* 44, no. 3 (April 1950).

MONTANA

The Slaughter of the Buffalo and The Hard Winter

Conklin, Dave. *Montana History Weekends: 52 Adventures in History.* Guilford, CT: Globe Pequot Press, 2002.

Fritz, Harry W., Mary Murphy, and Robert R. Swartout. *Montana Legacy: Essays on History, People, and Place.* Helena: Montana Historical Society Press, 2002.

Johanek, Durrae and John. *Montana Folks.* Helena: TwoDot, 2004.

Van West, Carroll. *Traveler's Companion to Montana History.* Helena: Montana Historical Society Press, 1986.

GLACIER NATIONAL PARK

Grinnell's Single Shot

Buchholtz, C. W. *Man in Glacier.* Glacier Natural History Association, 1976.

Grant, Madison. *Early History of Glacier National Park.* Washington, DC: Government Printing Office, 1919.

NEBRASKA

Homesteading

Creigh, Dorothy Weyer. *Nebraska.* Nashville, TN: American Association for State and Local History, 1977.

Orphan Train

Endorf, Charlotte M. *Plains Bound: Fragile Cargo.* Denver: Outskirts Press, 2005.

NEVADA

Building the Transcontinental Railroad

Ambrose, Steven E. *Nothing Like It in the World.* New York: Simon & Schuster, 2000.

Kraus, George. "Chinese Laborers and the Construction of the Central Pacific." *Utah Historical Quarterly* 37, no. 1 (Winter 1969): 41–57.

Railroaders. New York: Time-Life Books, 1973.

Utley, Robert M., and Francis A. Ketterson Jr. *Golden Spike National Historic Site.* Washington DC: National Park Service, 1992.

Absalom Lehman Discovers a Cave

Lehman Caves History, National Park Service. www.nps.gov/grba/history culture/lehman-caves-history.htm.

LAS VEGAS

Mormons Arrive in Las Vegas

Church of Jesus Christ of Latter Day Saints website: www.lds.org, www .lds.org/churchhistory/history.

Land, Barbara and Myrick. *A Short History of Las Vegas.* 2nd ed. Reno: University of Nevada Press, 2004.

Mormon Historic Sites Registry website: www.mormonhistoricsites.org, www.mormonhistoricsites.org/old-mormon-fort/.

National Park Service website: www.nps.gov, www.nps.gov/nr/twhp/ wwwlps/lessons/122fort/index.htm.

Nevada History website: www.nevada-history.org.

Nevada Division of State Parks website: www.parks.nv.gov, www.parks .nv.gov/olvmf.htm.

Old Las Vegas Mormon Fort State Historic Park, personal visit and observations by the author.

Vegas.com website: www.vegas.com/attractions, www.vegas.com/attrac tions/off_the_strip/mormonfort.html.

NEW MEXICO

Showdown in Las Vegas and The Death of Billy the Kid

Bryan, Howard. *Wildest of the Wild West.* Santa Fe: Clear Light Publishers, 1988.

Garrett, Pat. *The Authentic Life of Billy, the Kid.* Norman: University of Oklahoma Press, 1954.

Horan, James D. *Pictorial History of the Wild West.* New York: Crown Publishers, 1954.

Metz, Leon C. *The Shooters.* El Paso: Mangan Books, 1976.

Thrapp, Dan L. *Encyclopedia of Frontier Biography.* Glendale, CA: The Arthur H. Clark Company, 1988.

OKLAHOMA

After the Tears

Foreman, Grant. *Indian Removal: The Emigration of the Five Civilized Tribes of Indians.* Norman: University of Oklahoma Press, 1972.

Gregg, Josiah. *Commerce of the Prairies.* 1844. Reprint, Norman: University of Oklahoma Press, 1954.

Kansas Historical Society. "First Kansas Colored Infantry," in *Kansapedia.* Topeka, KS, 2010; www.kshs.org/kansapedia/first-kansas-col ored-infantry/12052.

McLoughlin, William G. *After the Trail of Tears: The Cherokees' Struggle for Sovereignty, 1839–1880.* Chapel Hill: University of North Carolina Press, 1993.

Perdue, Theda. *Slavery and the Evolution of Cherokee Society, 1540–1866.* Knoxville: University of Tennessee Press, 1979.

Thornton, Russell. *The Cherokees: A Population History.* Lincoln: University of Nebraska Press, 1990.

Boomer Sooner

Baldwin, Kathlyn. *The 89ers: Oklahoma Land Rush of 1889.* Oklahoma City: Western Heritage Books, 1981.

"The Chief Boomer Shot." *New York Times,* April 5, 1890.

Hoig, Stan. *The Oklahoma Land Run of 1889.* Oklahoma City: Oklahoma Historical Society, 1989.

Thompson, John. *Closing the Frontier: Radical Response in Oklahoma, 1889–1923.* Norman: University of Oklahoma Press, 1986.

Welsh, Carol H. "Deadly Games: The Struggle for a Quarter-section of Land." *Chronicles of Oklahoma* 52, no. 1 (Spring 1994): 36–51.

OREGON

The Great Migration

Burnett, Peter H. *Recollections and Opinions of an Old Pioneer.* New York: 1880.

Edwards, P. L. *Sketch of the Oregon Territory or, Emigrants' Guide.* Liberty, MO: Printed at the *Herald* Office, 1842.

Morgan, Dale. *Jedediah Smith and the Opening of the West.* Indianapolis: The Bobbs-Merrill Company, Inc., 1953.

Making Headlines Oregon-Style

Karolevitz, Robert F. *Newspapering in the Old West.* Seattle: Superior Publishing Company, 1965. Reprinted by Bonanza Books, New York, nd.

SOUTH DAKOTA

Todd the Lobbyist: Dakota Territory Is Established

Barbour, Barton H. *Fort Union and the Upper Missouri Fur Trade.* Norman: University of Oklahoma Press, 2001.

Lamar, Howard. *Dakota Territory, 1861–1889: A Study of Frontier Politics.* New Haven, CT: Yale University Press, 1956.

———, ed. *The New Encyclopedia of the American West.* New Haven, CT: Yale University Press, 1998.

Smith, George Martin, ed. *History of Dakota Territory—South Dakota: Its History and Its People,* Vol. II. Chicago: The S. J. Clarke Publishing Company, 1915.

The Death of a Legend: Sitting Bull's Last Days

Allison, Edwin Henry. *The Surrender of Sitting Bull.* Charleston, SC: BiblioLife, 2008.

Anderson, Gary. *Sitting Bull and the Paradox of Lakota Nationhood*, 2nd ed. White Plains, NY: Longman, 2006.

Brown, Dee. *Bury My Heart at Wounded Knee: An Indian History of the American West.* New York: Henry Holt & Company, 2001.

Roop, Peter, and Connie Roop. *Sitting Bull.* New York: Scholastic Paperbacks, 2002.

Viola, Herman. *Trail to Wounded Knee: The Last Stand of the Plains Indians, 1860–1890.* Washington, DC: National Geographic Society, 2003.

Yenne, Bill. *Sitting Bull.* Yardley, PA: Westholme Publishing, 2009.

TEXAS

A Cargo of Camels

Boyd, Eva Jolene. *Noble Brutes: Camels on the American Frontier.* Plano: Republic of Texas Press, 1995.

Billy Dixon's Remarkable Shot

Botkin, B. A., ed. *A Treasury of Western Folklore.* New York: Wings Books, 1975.

Earle, Jim. "Billy Dixon and the Mile-Long Shot," in *America: The Men and Their Guns That Made Her Great.* Los Angeles: Petersen Publishing, 1981.

Englert, Steve. "Billy Dixon: Plainsman Supreme," in *1995 Dixie Gun Works Blackpowder Annual.* Union City, TN: Pioneer Press, 1994.

Utley, Robert M. *The Indian Frontier and the American West; 1846–1890.* Albuquerque: University of New Mexico Press, 1984.

SAN ANTONIO

Rough Riding

Campbell, Randolph B. *Gone to Texas: A History of the Lone Star State.* New York: Oxford University Press, 2003.

Daughters of the Republic of Texas. *The Wall of History: The History of the Alamo.* San Antonio: The Daughters of the Republic of Texas.

Williams, Docia Schultz. *The History and Mystery of the Menger Hotel.* Lanham, MD: Republic of Texas Press, 2000.

UTAH

Driving the Golden Spike

Alexander, Thomas G. *Utah: The Right Place.* Salt Lake City: Gibbs Smith, Publisher, 1995.

Martha Hughes Cannon Wins a Race

White, Jean Bickmore. "Martha H. Cannon." In *Sister Saints: Women in Early Utah.* Edited by Vicky Burgess-Olson. Provo, Utah: Brigham Young University, 1978.

WASHINGTON

Indian Wars

Dodd, Jack. "The Indians Have an Inning." *Great Western Indian Fights.* Compiled by Potomac Corral of the Westerners. Lincoln: University of Nebraska Press, n.d.

Utley, Robert M., and Wilcomb E. Washburn. *The American Heritage History of the Indian Wars.* New York: American Heritage Publishing Co., 1977.

SEATTLE

Here Come the Brides

Andrews, Mildred Tanner. *Pioneer Square: Seattle's Oldest Neighborhood.* Seattle: University of Washington Press, 2005.

Lange, Greg. "Mercer Girls Reach Seattle on May 16, 1864." History Link.org Essay 166, November 1998. www.historylink.org/index .cfm?DisplayPage=output.cfm&file_id=166.

Morgan, Murray. *Skid Road*. Seattle: University of Washington Press, 1951.

Muhich, Peri. "Mercer Girls." HistoryLink.org Essay 1125, May 1999. www.historylink.org/index.cfm?DisplayPage=output.cfm&file_ id=1125.

Speidel, William C., *Sons of the Profits*. Seattle: Nettle Creek Publishing Company, 1967.

Stein, Alan J. "*Here Come the Brides* debuts on ABC on September 25, 1968." HistoryLink.org Essay 1563, January 1999. www.historylink .org/index.cfm?DisplayPage=output.cfm&file_id=1563.

Warren, James R. *King County and its Queen City: Seattle*. Woodland Hills, CA: Windsor Publications Inc., 1981.

———. *Seattle: 150 Years of Progress*. Carlsbad, CA: Heritage Media Group, 2001.

WYOMING

A Historic Vote

Architect of the Capitol website: www.aoc.gov/cc/art/nsh/morris.cfm.

Brown, Larry K. *Coyotes and Canaries: Characters Who Made the West Wild . . . and Wonderful*. Glendo, WY: High Plains Press, 2002.

Library of Congress website: www.loc.gov/rr/program/bib/our docs/13thamendment.html.

Library of Congress website: www.loc.gov/rr/program/bib/ourdocs/ Louisiana.html.

Made in Wyoming: Our Legacy of Success website: www.madeinwyo ming.net/profiles/morris.php.

National Susan B. Anthony Museum and House website: http://susanb anthonyhouse.org/her-story/biography.php#suff.

South Pass City State Historic Site website: www.southpasscity.com.

State of Wyoming website: http://wyoming.gov/chronology.aspx.

State of Wyoming website: http://wyoming.gov/history.aspx.

Women of the West Museum website: http://theautry.org/

Wyoming State Archives website: http://wyoarchives.state.wy.us.

The Johnson County War

Ancestry.com website, "Johnson County War": www.rootsweb.ancestry .com/~wytttp/history/johnson/Johnsoncounty1.htm.

Davis, John W. *Wyoming Range War: The Infamous Invasion of Johnson County.* Norman: University of Oklahoma Press. Kindle Edition (2011-11-19).

Day, Brian. *Wyoming Trivia: The Most Incredible, Unbelievable, Wild, Weird, Fun, Fascinating, and True Facts About Wyoming!* Helena, MT: Riverbend Publishing, 2008.

Johnson County, Wyoming, website: www.johnsoncountywyoming.org.

National Park Service website, "Abraham Lincoln and the West": www .nps.gov/home/historyculture/lincolnandwest.htm.

Wilson, Michael R. *Outlaw Tales of Wyoming: True Stories of the Cowboy State's Most Infamous Crooks, Culprits, and Cutthroats.* Guilford, CT: Morris Book Publishing, 2008.

Wyoming Tales and Trails website, "Johnson County War": www.wyo mingtalesandtrails.com/johnson.html.

YELLOWSTONE NATIONAL PARK

Emma Cowan and the Nez Perce

Josephy, Alvin M. Jr. *Chief Joseph's People and Their War.* The Yellowstone Association for Natural Science, History, and Education, 1964.

Kauffman, Polly Wells. *National Parks and the Woman's Voice, A History.* Albuquerque: University of New Mexico Press, 1996.

Miller, Mark M. *Adventures in Yellowstone.* Guilford, CT: TwoDot, 2009.

Walter, Dave. *Montana Campfire Tales.* Helena, MT: Falcon Publishing, 1996.

THE LEWIS AND CLARK EXPEDITION

Grizzly Encounters

Ambrose, Stephen E. *Undaunted Courage: Meriwether Lewis, Thomas Jefferson, and the Opening of the American West.* New York: Simon & Schuster, 1996.

DeVoto, Bernard, ed. *The Journals of Lewis and Clark.* Boston: Houghton Mifflin, 1953.

Fifer, Barbara and Vicky Soderberg. *Along the Trail with Lewis and Clark.* Helena: Montana Magazine, 1998.

Gold Thwaites, Reuben, ed. *Original Journals of the Lewis and Clark Expedition.* New York: Dodd, Mead and Company, 1905.

Schullery, Paul. *Lewis and Clark among the Grizzlies.* Helena, MT: Falcon Publishing, 2002.

THE OREGON TRAIL

The Last Great Challenge: The Barlow Road

Belshaw, Maria Parsons. *Crossing the Plains to Oregon in 1853.* Fairfield, WA: Ye Galleon Press, 2000.

Fanselow, Julie. *Traveling the Oregon Trail.* Guilford, CT: Globe Pequot Press, 2001.

Luchetti, Cathy. *Women of the West.* New York: Orion Books, 1982.

Schlissel, Lillian. *Women's Diaries of the Westward Journey.* New York: Schocken Books, 1982, 1992.

THE SANTA FE TRAIL

A Winter Crossing of the Prairie

Dary, David. *The Santa Fe Trail: Its History, Legends and Lore.* New York: Alfred A. Knopf, 2001.

Duffus, R. L. *The Santa Fe Trail.* Albuquerque: University of New Mexico, 1972.

SOURCES

It Happened in Alaska, by Diane Olthuis

It Happened in Arizona, 3rd edition, by James Crutchfield

It Happened at Grand Canyon, 2nd edition, by Todd R. Berger

It Happened in Northern California, 2nd edition, by Erin H. Turner

It Happened in San Francisco, by Maxine Cass

It Happened in Yosemite National Park, by Ray Jones and Joe Lubow

It Happened in Southern California, by Noelle Sullivan

It Happened in Colorado, 3rd edition, by James Crutchfield

It Happened in Denver, by Stephen Grace

It Happened in Rocky Mountain National Park, by Phyllis Perry

It Happened in Idaho, by Randy Stapilus

It Happened in Kansas, by Sarah Smarsh

It Happened in Missouri, 2nd edition, by Sean McLachlan

It Happened in Montana, 3rd edition, by James Crutchfield

It Happened in Glacier National Park, 2nd edition, by Vince Moravek

It Happened in Nebraska, by Tammy Partsch

It Happened in Nevada, 2nd edition, by Elizabeth Gibson

It Happened in Las Vegas, by Paul W. Papa

It Happened in New Mexico, 2nd edition, by James Crutchfield

It Happened in Oklahoma, 2nd edition, by Robert Dorman

It Happened in Oregon, 2nd edition, by James Crutchfield

SOURCES

It Happened in South Dakota, 2nd edition, by Patrick Straub and T. D. Griffith

It Happened in Texas, 3rd edition, by James Crutchfield

It Happened in San Antonio, by Marilyn Bennett Alexander

It Happened in Utah, 2nd edition, by Tom and Gayen Wharton

It Happened in Washington, 3rd edition, by James Crutchfield

It Happened in Seattle, by Steve Pomper

It Happened in Wyoming, by Paul W. Papa

It Happened in Yellowstone National Park, 2nd edition, by Erin H. Turner

It Happened on the Lewis and Clark Expedition, 2nd edition, by Erin H. Turner

It Happened on the Oregon Trail, 2nd edition, by Tricia Martineau-Wagner

It Happened on the Santa Fe Trail, by Stephen Glassman

INDEX